MW00876622

PROVEN GENUINE

AN EXAMINATION OF SUFFERING IN
THE BOOK OF JOB

DR. ANDREW N. SMELLIE

PROVEN GENUINE

AN EXAMINATION OF SUFFERING IN THE BOOK OF JOB

Please email the author at Andrew@usd21.org.

Editor-in-Chief: Dr. Kip McKean

Cover credit: Jake Studer

ISBN: 9798667683247

Due to print on demand technology, edits and corrections
can continue to be made to this document. Please send any
corrections, comments or suggestions to the author as they
are greatly appreciated.

ENDORSEMENTS

Dr. Raul Moreno
São Paulo Lead Evangelist and World Sector Leader of Latin America

"Suffering" is the universal equalizer! It does not discriminate with age, gender, race, nationality or social status. Dr. Andrew Smellie, my great friend and fellow missionary, gifts his audience with exceptional insights into this topic by "deglossing" the amazing yet often misunderstood Book of Job! A great read for anyone who has suffered... That is everyone!

Joe Willis
Sydney Lead Evangelist and World Sector Leader of Austral-China

With real life heroes and relevant stories, the account of Job comes to life. Andrew masterfully expands on the main issues, questions and grievances in man's heart towards God in Job's times and our times today. Are you in pain? Read this book. Are you feeling misunderstood? Read this book. Are you finding it hard to understand God's plan for your life? Read this book. Thank you, Andrew, for daring to address the questions others want to avoid.

John A. Causey III

Chicago Lead Evangelist and Geographic Sector Leader of the PACK Churches

The principle goal of every book is to fulfill the intention for which it was written. Andrew's vision to instill spiritual vigor to this generation and the next is emulated in *Proven Genuine*. It is indeed not only a riveting and provocative study on the life and suffering of Job, but provides integral insights on the character of God. His moving personal accounts and profound sparring analogies exhilarate readers to fight for discipleship. I believe Andrew's testimony and shared conviction is critical for raising up the fighters for the future!

Michael Williamson

London Lead Evangelist and World Sector Leader of Europe

"Holy through hardship; a fragile emotional state can make us question Biblical truths; and it is when the trials of life come that we must remember the promises of God" are just a few of an unlimited colorful array of modern-day proverbs, that can instantly bring healing to the most hurting individual. Andrew gives an excellent exposition and perspective for some of life's most profound questions through an overview study of the Book of Job. Congratulations, my dear brother Andrew, your book is masterful, and a must-read primer for ministry!

Blaise Feumba
Abidjan Lead Evangelist and Geographic Sector Leader of French Africa
This book is a masterpiece! Great job Andrew and thanks for using your writing skills and profound insights to help all of us to better understand God's greater purposes behind the sufferings he allows us to go through. Your thought-provoking questions throughout this treatise led me to a deeper trust of God and his molding of me into a noble vessel to accomplish his purposes in the nations.

Nick Bordieri
The Phnom Penh MERCY Orphanage Director and World Sector Leader of MERCY
Dr. Andrew Smellie, a dear friend and partner in the gospel, does a marvelous job addressing some of life's most challenging questions in *Proven Genuine*. Indeed, Dr. Smellie is one who exemplifies the genuine faith about which he has written. Page after page, you will be called higher as you learn through Job's trials to suffer with grace, perseverance and integrity.

Helen Sullivan

Orlando Women's Ministry Leader and Woman World Sector Leader of Eastern USA and South Asia

In *Proven Genuine,* Dr. Andrew Smellie masterfully explains the truths of one of the most misunderstood books of the Bible – the Book of Job. The Book of Job is brought to life, as Dr. Smellie weaves in stories from his personal journey, as well as so many inspiring stories from his years of missionary work in the continent of Africa. It is a must read if you want to gain a better understanding of the nature of God and why there is suffering in our world.

Michael Kirchner

Los Angeles Shepherd and World Sector Leader of Administration and Law

In *Proven Genuine,* Andrew skillfully guides us to an understanding that we each will face tests in our lives and suffering is a part of our Christian journey. Each of us can seek comfort in the knowledge that God has a purpose in mind during our trials – that our faith is "proven genuine." As Andrew shares, you will find a helpful summary of the "do's and don'ts" in "giving and receiving" discipling in our lives. Please grab your Bible, turn to the Book of Job, and read *Proven Genuine.*

LuJack Martinez
Washington DC Lead Evangelist
If you are a Christian going through a rough time in your walk with God, Dr. Andrew Smellie's *Proven Genuine* is a book that will enlighten, inspire and encourage you to keep fighting the good fight with all your heart. If you are a serious student of the Bible, you will greatly benefit from Dr. Smellie's insightful analysis of this timeless book. Yet if you are prayerfully considering God's call into the full-time Christian ministry, I recommend you not only buy this amazing book, but keep it next to your most valuable reference materials – because herein you will find not just theory, but actual, practical real-life lessons gleaned from the daily application of the Holy Scriptures by a proven practitioner on the mission field.

Dr. Tim Kernan
Los Angeles Lead Evangelist and Pacific Rim World Sector Leader
Dr. Andrew Smellie, a dear friend, has written a much-needed book on suffering and the divine purposes of hardships and difficulties. With Scriptural guidance accompanied by inspiring illustrations, Andrew helps us to understand how God tests the integrity, the endurance and the character of those he loves through trials of many kinds! This is a must read for every disciple. Thank you Andrew!

Elena Sirotkina
Women's Ministry Leader of Kiev and the
Eurasian World Sector

As a Ukrainian woman in this age of great political chaos, I welcome this amazing Bible study on suffering in the Book of Job. I pray that the light that Andrew shone on the trials and tribulations of Job will guide the understandings of this generation and the ones to come to see God's hand in sufferings and persecutions. I highly recommend this ground-breaking book to all Christians in all nations as we all are facing the attacks of Satan.

Tony Untalan
Movement Shepherd and World Sector Leader of Shepherding

Proven Genuine by Dr Andrew Smellie gives us a look at life's sufferings and the needed perseverance to endure from the Biblical perspective of Job's life. No one likes to suffer. While very few people will face the intense sufferings that Job experienced, the reality of our level of suffering is to us at times equally challenging. This insightful manuscript has so many Scriptures and practicals to give hope to the hopeless, and also helps us to see the healing side that suffering will bring. As a Shepherd, I beg you to please read this book. This book changed my life and it might possibly change yours!

DEDICATION

*I am forever indebted to God for the privilege
of suffering as a disciple of Jesus Christ, and for
the blessing of my faithful, spiritual and beautiful
wife, Patrique. The gifts of our two adorable children,
Naomi and Isaiah, have been our greatest treasures.
Without my wife's loving support to hold our two
strong-willed children at bay, this book could
never have been written. She is a godsend
and will always be the love of my life.*

*"But he knows the way that I take; when
he has tested me, I will come forth as gold."*
Job 23:10

*"In this you greatly rejoice, though now for a little
while you may have had to suffer grief in all kinds of
trials. These have come so that your faith – of greater
worth than gold, which perishes even though refined by
fire – may be proved genuine and may result in praise,
glory and honor when Jesus Christ is revealed."*
1 Peter 1:6-7

"People are like tea bags. You don't know their
flavor… until they are put in hot water." - Eila Smellie
(A common expression by the mother of the author)

"Tomorrow if all literature was to be destroyed and
it was left to me to retain one work only, I would save
[the Book of] Job." - Victor Hugo (19th century
French poet and author)

CONTENTS

FOREWARD

Andrew's favorite Scripture is Proverbs 16:9, *"In his heart a man plans his course, but the Lord determines his steps!"* This so describes Andrew's amazing life! Raised by outstanding parents, Andrew fulfilled his ambitious "plans" by being accepted into Cornell University – one of the eight prestigious Ivy League Colleges in America! He received scholarships for both his Bachelor of Science Degree in Health and Society (2001) and his Master's of Health Administration (2003). However, "unplanned" was his baptism on May 20, 2000! The Lord determined Andrew's next step, as he called Andrew into the full-time ministry in Syracuse, New York in late 2003! It was a few months later in June 2004 at the Portland World Missions Jubilee that I first met this talented young man about whom I had heard so much! Afterall, as a "baby Christian" Andrew distinguished himself, as he would travel one and one half hours each way to church... in the winter through snow storms!

During Elena's and my three and a half years in Portland from July 2003 to January 2007, many brothers and sisters "backed off" being our friends because of our continued radical call for the International Churches of Christ (ICOC) to return to discipling, central leadership and the dream of the evangelization of the nations in this generation. Yet Andrew and his new bride Patrique – who were married on August 6, 2005 – never flinched when the Portland ICOC Church, Elena and I were disfellowshipped in October 2005 by 85 of the "most renowned" preachers and elders in what was left of the ICOC around the world. In fact, I saw in both Andrew and Patrique a rare love for God expressed in their love for the truth, their embracing of God forming a new movement, and their growing friendship with Elena and me.

In 2008, I asked Andrew and Patrique to lead the planting of the Washington DC Church. As one of the first plantings of the SoldOut Discipling Movement, this congregation was heavily persecuted, yet the church grew quickly. Then at the 2009 Winter Workshop in Syracuse (five years before "World Sector Leaders" were chosen), Elena and I had Sunday lunch with Andrew and Patrique and asked them to oversee the evangelization of Africa. Andrew was elated; Patrique cried. She cried because she knew in part the heavy price of leaving loved ones behind in order to serve as missionaries in the third world. Yet, she too agreed that very day that this was the Lord determining the Smellies' steps.

By 2010, I invited Andrew and Patrique to move to LA so that we could work side by side in the gospel. It was during this time that God blessed the Smellies with "my" beautiful granddaughter Naomi on January 2, 2011. In July 2011, I sent the Smellies to rescue, stabilize and grow the young New York City Church. There my awesome grandson Isaiah was born on December 15, 2012.

The Smellies returned to LA in 2014, where they became the "Africanus" World Sector Leaders over the continent of Africa and the Mid-Atlantic USA States. Of course, their main purpose in returning was to prepare to plant in 2016 our vision for the "pillar church" of Africa – Johannesburg, South Africa. Yet, in 2015 while Andrew and I were in Abidjan, Ivory Coast for the First African Missions Conference, we studied with a Mainline Church of Christ preacher – Dr. Benedict Atason – who had traveled by bus from Nigeria through four African nations just to meet us and join the SoldOut Movement.

Upon "Ben" visiting Los Angeles a few months later, as the Man of Macedonia in a dream guided Paul to expand his vision from Asia to Europe, so Ben became the "Man of Nigeria" persuading both Andrew and me to come to Lagos instead of Johannesburg as there was so much opportunity for the gospel. Andrew heard God's "determined" voice once again, and so in June 2016, Andrew and Patrique along with nine other valiant disciples planted the Lagos International Christian Church! Two months later, in August 2016, I was very honored to "hood" Andrew as only the fourth recipient of the International College of Christian Ministry Doctorate Degree!

Kip hooded the author for his ICCM Doctorate of Ministry Degree at the 2016 Global Leadership Conference in LA!

Three years later, after battling the third world challenges of constant sickness, physical persecutions and visa complications, this vibrant congregation had multiplied to 155 disciples!

Well, as one can see from Andrew's life, it is true that the Lord determines one's steps. Yet, when one *"[takes] delight in the Lord, God will give you the delight of your heart."* (Psalm 37:4) So, on June 2019, the Spirit carried Andrew and Patrique from Lagos to Johannesburg. In September at the Johannesburg Inaugural Service, Elena and I were reunited with our beloved son and daughter in the faith and of course our grandchildren – Naomi and Isaiah! As of today, the Spirit – working through the Smellie's extraordinary prayerful and skillful leadership – has grown the work in Africa to five planted churches and 13 remnant groups in 13 nations totalling 1,500 disciples! As Paul said of Timothy, I can say of Andrew, *"I have no one else like him... You know that [Andrew] has proved himself, because as a son with his father he served with me in the work of the gospel."* (Philippians 2:20-22) This profound book – *Proven Genuine - An Examination Of Suffering In The Book Of Job* – has it's genesis in Andrew's doctoral dissertation on the Book of Job, as well as Andrew's personal sufferings in the evangelization of Africa. After reading this book, may God bless you to live out your Christian life with the integrity of Job and Andrew.

We are family... filled with visions and dreams,
Dr. Kip McKean
Los Angeles, California
July 19, 2020

PREFACE AND ACKNOWLEDGEMENTS

"God is our refuge and strength, an ever-present help in trouble." (Psalm 46:1)

The inspiration for this book was due in part to a valiant brother in the faith, Erick Homiak, who went home to be with the Lord on August 26, 2015. Despite numerous health challenges and a tragic accident in rehabilitation that left him a quadriplegic, Erick's example of being "patient in affliction" before his passing encouraged the entire West Region of the City of Angels International Christian Church. (Romans 12:12)

In June 2016, I was given an opportunity to be "proven genuine" along with my wife Patrique and nine other mission team members, as the Holy Spirit guided us to plant a discipling church in Lagos, Nigeria – the largest city in Africa with 21,000,000 lost souls. For the three glorious years that my family and I served the Lord in Lagos, I was personally moved by the resilence of the Lagos disciples and their love for God, as we overcame the "wahala" (Nigerian expression for "drama") of third world living – consistently dealing with malaria, typhoid, unclean water, inconsistent electricity, police extortion and reckless drivers with smiles on our faces! I thank God for dear "sons in the faith" like Joshua Ajayi, Tolani Abiodun and Osas Atohengbe who raised up to become powerful men of God in Lagos and later accompanied me to Johannesburg, South Africa!

The friendship of a dear Nigerian brother, Goodhope Atason, was also a great support as he led the handful of souls in the Lagos Remnant Group before the Lagos Mission Team's arrival, thus making our transition from the United States to Nigeria as smooth as possible. He has continued to serve as the very capable Administrator for the Lagos Church. His father, Dr. Benedict Atason, is affectionately called the *"Man of Macedonia"* for Nigeria, as he sold his possessions to gain the funds necessary to travel from Nigeria to the Ivory Coast to attend our First African Missions Conference in 2015! (Acts 16:9) His conviction to *"discern what is best"* – as a former Mainline Church of Christ preacher who joined God's New Movement – served to light a fire for the entire African continent and beyond! (Philippians 1:9-11)

Special thanks are also due to Jacques and Jeanette Groenewald, who began the remnant group in Johannesburg and waited in anticipation for almost four years as the Johannesburg Mission Team's arrival was changed due to our obedience to the "Macedonian Call" from Nigeria. (Acts 16:7-10) Their faith in God and love for their native land inspired them to give up the comforts of London and their "home church" in November 2015 to prepare the foundation for the Johannesburg Church Planting. Nick Winn, a dear Afrikaans brother who joined us from our former fellowship, has also been instrumental in gathering God's remnant in South Africa and has now become a "right-hand man" for me in Johannesburg. Patrique and I also appreciate the support and sacrifice of our other Johannesburg Mission Team Members – Chris and Lerato Wooden, Ariel Atohengbe, Kate Abiodun, Tina Nwachukwu and Shyloe Pollard – as we have worked together to build the mighty Johannesburg Church!

By the grace of God, our efforts to evangelize the Africanus World Sector (Africa and Mid-Atlantic USA) will be accomplished through the friendship and faith of our Pillar Church Leaders: Blaise and Patricia Feumba of Abidjan, Ivory Coast; Bolaji and Chinyere Akinfenwa of Lagos, Nigeria; Micky and Lyly Ngungu of Kinshasa, Democratic Republic of Congo; and LuJack and Cathi Martinez of Washington, DC. The recent challenges of COVID-19 Pandemic on the

African continent have been difficult, yet these faithful men and women continue to *"shine like stars"* as they serve and lead God's great people. (Philippians 2:14-16) The generosity of our sister congregation in Washington DC continues to refresh our hearts. This church will always be dear to us as this was the first church that Patrique and I were honored to plant in 2008.

Patrique and I are also very grateful for the love, support and prayers of the World Sector Leaders Council, as they constantly live out what we all pledged to one another during our first communion on August 6, 2014: *"We are family... to the end!"* (Revelation 2:26) We believe that the faith and courage of this "band of brothers and sisters" will accomplish Jesus' dream to *"make disciples of all nations"* in THIS generation! (Matthew 28:19) Thanks also is due to the diligent efforts of Dr. Cheryl Harris-Chin, Jeanne McGee, Sharon Kirchner and the team at SoldOut Press International to thoroughly edit this manuscript when my eyes were too tired to read it again!

Finally, I thank God daily for the spiritual guidance and friendship of Drs. Kip and Elena McKean. Their courageous example and call to rebuild the standard of Biblical Christianity is unprecedented in our time. It is an honor to imitate their faith as they are father and mother in the faith to Patrique and me, and grandparents to Naomi and Isaiah.

In his service,
Dr. Andrew N. Smellie, D.Min.
Johannesburg, South Africa
July 15, 2020

INTRODUCTION: THE
SPIRITUAL BOXING RING

Life is like a boxing match: Defeat is declared not when you fall, but when you refuse to stand up again.
- Anonymous

Though a first degree black belt in Goju-Ryu Karate, the author (red shorts) enjoyed his Dutch Kickboxing Class in Los Angeles in 2015!

The Book of Job is one of the greatest literary works of all time. This timeless book is regarded by many Biblical scholars as one of the first books of the Patriarchal Era before the Mosaic Law.[1] This account of Job's life can be considered a historical "boxing match" of sorts, as it explores the "spiritual fight" of Job versus the malicious schemes of Satan. Job faces the challenge of battling his own emotions and the

---

[1] Halley, Henry H (1927, 1965). *Halley's Bible Handbook.* Zondervan Publishing House.

23

misguided "wounds" by friends, with God as the ultimate "referee."

This concept of a spiritual battle is also portrayed in 1 Corinthians 9, as Paul of Tarsus – the Apostle to the Gentiles – compares the Christian lifestyle to the self-discipline and strict training required for a successful runner or boxer. While the goal of training for a first-century athlete was to win the coveted "crown" of fig leaves for a season, the goal of training for the Christian "athlete" is to obtain a *"crown that will last forever"* – the salvation of our souls through eternal life in Christ! (1 Corinthians 9:25)   In his epistle, James – the half-brother of Jesus – states, *"Blessed is the one who perseveres under trial because, having stood the test, that person will receive the crown of life that the Lord has promised to those who love him."* (James 1:12)

The Book of Job is a powerful case study of suffering through spiritual trials, as we see the valiant struggle of one man to overcome his extraordinary circumstances with faith, perseverance and integrity. Since this epic struggle is recorded in 42 chapters of God's Holy Scriptures, the examination of Job's sufferings must become equally important for every disciple of Jesus. Afterall, every disciple faces a "daily fight" to be righteous in the sight of God through the trials of life. Through the inspiration of the Spirit, the Apostle Paul also describes how every Christian athlete can be successful in their own spiritual battle.

> *Therefore I do not run uncertainly [without definite aim]. I do not box like one beating the air and striking without an adversary. But [like a boxer] I buffet my body [handle it roughly, discipline it by hardships] and subdue it, for fear that after proclaiming to others the gospel and things pertaining to it, I myself should become unfit [not stand the test, be unapproved and*

rejected as a counterfeit]. (1 Corinthians 9:26-27 AMP)

The Amplified Version of this passage calls our attention to the need for spiritual training. Without making the effort to ***"buffet"*** our bodies, we can become undisciplined for the task ahead. If our personal righteousness falls short, it would be an embarrassment to us and hypocritical to those around us. Jesus originally laid out this challenge to ***"count the cost"*** for every person who desires to become his disciple.

> ***Suppose one of you wants to build a tower. Won't you first sit down and estimate the cost to see if you have enough money to complete it? For if you lay the foundation and are not able to finish it, everyone who sees it will ridicule you, saying, "This person began to build and wasn't able to finish."*** (Luke 14:28-30)

Our goal must be ***"to finish."*** Every year millions of people make "New Year's Resolutions" that are never completed, because they either give up or lose track of their plans. Similarly, as Jesus' disciples, we must remember that "to die faithful in Christ" is the goal of our Christian walk. "Spiritual athletes" understand that their prize is the crown of eternal life in Jesus Christ. As a result, our discipleship is not for mere pretense, like a boxer only practicing in mid-air without any intent to actually enter the ring. Our discipleship is to prepare us to die faithful and hear the Lord say, ***"Well done, good and faithful servant!"*** (Matthew 25:21) But what is this training process to "buffet" ourselves all about?

A Martial Arts Perspective

In the famous martial arts film, *Enter The Dragon* (1973), the character O'Hara (played by Bob Wall) holds up a board in front of Bruce Lee's face and breaks it with a punch. Lee stares back unblinkingly and says, slowly and emphatically,

"Boards… don't hit back." Most martial art enthusiasts understand today that hitting a "dead" target (a board or punching bag) does not necessarily mean you will be able to hit someone who is actively resisting your attack. In order to be a good fighter, you need to do more than practice hitting things that "don't hit back."

Most martial arts training drills have a high degree of predictability due to its "static" or non-dynamic environment. These exercises start from a stationary position and end in a stationary position. So in a drill, barring any mistakes or carelessness, the situation is entirely predictable. However, in reality, fighting (of any kind) is a process of constant, chaotic change. It is a dynamic environment where usually both or if there are multiple opponents, all of you are in motion. More than that, you and your opponent(s) are likely to be accelerating. In other words, you not only have the vectors and velocity of your own movements and your attackers' movements to consider, but also the way in which these vectors and velocities are changing. In short, nothing about real fighting is predictable.

In order to apply static training to a dynamic environment, the answer lies in sparring – what is sometimes called "live training," or training against "resistant partners." In sparring, you face your partner and actually start "fighting." Not "real fighting," but a kind of "play fighting" where the rules of engagement are sufficient to protect you both from real injury, while leaving sufficient physical stress to "test your skill." As your skill level increases, so does the intensity level of your sparring.

How does all of this relate for a "spiritual martial artist?" Our daily discipline of Bible study and prayer is an example of static or non-dynamic training. We use the skills that we have learned through our reliance on God and His word in the static environment of our "quiet times" and apply it to the dynamic environment of the world. By incorporating the perfect standard of the Bible as we deal with the temptations of society (lust, materialism, anger, etc.), we will be equipped for the "spiritual sparring" that occurs when we share our faith and deal with the responses or "attacks" in return! For a spiritual athlete, the training of spiritual sparring is necessary to determine how effective and productive our static training (convictions gained from our quiet time) has been to endure and prevail in a real spiritual battle. As a result, the lack of effectiveness and weaknesses that are exposed through this spiritual sparring can be analyzed by a coach (discipling partner) and turned into strengths.

The skills gained from spiritual sparring to defend and counterattack against the Devil's schemes along with the ability to teach others to do the same is an important indicator of spiritual growth. These factors distinguish those who are inexperienced in the *"elementary truths of God's word"* from those who are mature. (Hebrews 5:12) Spiritual maturity is proven genuine by those *"who by constant use have trained themselves to distinguish good from evil."* (Hebrews 5:14)

This *"constant use"* of God's word in spiritual training is not found by living in the typical "Hollywood" portrayal of Buddhist monks or Catholic priests in a monastery, far from the very people that Jesus calls us to save. That example is not the front-lines of spiritual battle, but rather the sidelines. While it is true that we all need our own "personal monasteries" – a place to focus on prayer and petition in order to engage the power of God – prayer without an outward focus on the ministry of the word is like *"faith without deeds."* (James 2:20) As a result, the Apostle Paul, speaking to his young protégé Timothy, the leader of the church in Ephesus, encouraged him to *"command certain people not to preach false doctrines any longer"* and to

27

use the word of God to admonish *"lawbreakers and rebels, the ungodly and the sinful, the unholy and the irreligious, for those who kill their fathers or mothers, for murderers, for the sexually immoral, for those practicing homosexuality, for slave traders and liars and perjurers – and for whatever else is contrary to the sound doctrine..."* (1 Timothy 1:3, 9-10) Paul understood that it is not enough to <u>know</u> the truth; the challenge is to <u>defend</u> it. As well in Acts 18:28, Apollos' skill on display as an experienced spiritual fighter, *"For he vigorously refuted his Jewish opponents in public debate, proving from the Scriptures that Jesus was the Messiah."*

Do you appreciate the importance of spiritual training? Do you desire to "fight the battle well, holding on to faith and a good conscience" or are you unaware that you need to *"buffet"* your body in order to train for battle? (1 Timothy 1:18) Paul admonishes his son in the faith Timothy by stating, *"Join with me in suffering, like a good soldier of Christ Jesus."* (2 Timothy 2:3) These passages remind us that spiritual, emotional and even physical hardships are an important element of our training as Christian warriors, so that our faith is tested and proven genuine by God. I was always inspired to note that the Lord is known for this example, as the Scriptures state in Exodus 15:3, *"The Lord is a warrior; the Lord is his name."*

Sadly, although Paul encouraged Timothy to *"fight the good fight of the faith,"* most modern Christians are woefully ignorant of what it means to *"fight"* at all; they are unaware that they have stepped into the "spiritual boxing ring" and Satan's crosshairs at their baptism into Christ! (1 Timothy 6:12) Interestingly, the Greek definition of the word *"fight"* means to "contend for a prize, struggle."[2] For many naïve Christians, the concept of a *"fight"* seems counterproductive to being a *"peacemaker."* (Matthew 5:9) As a result, many "Christians" are taken by surprise when they are "attacked or bruised" in the spiritual "boxing ring of faith," since they have not been engaged in strict training – the only way to become stronger in Christ.

So why do we need to fight spiritually? The Apostle Peter further confirms Paul's admonition to Timothy:

> **Be alert and of sober mind. Your enemy the devil prowls around like a roaring lion looking for someone to devour. Resist him, standing firm in the faith, because you know that the family of believers throughout the world is undergoing the same kind of sufferings.** (1 Peter 5:8)

Saying that we are faithful Christians is one thing; to prove our faith by standing firm and resisting the Devil through spiritual hardships is quite another! As the 19th century American philosopher Elbert Hubbard stated, "God will not look you over for medals, degrees or diplomas but for scars."[3]

In a discussion with Antoni Hardonik – a former UFC and K1 kickboxer and owner of Dynamix MMA in Los Angeles, California where I trained in kickboxing – I asked him for some insight regarding areas that needed improvement in my training. His response did not focus on a particular flaw in my fighting style. Instead, he said that the goal in progressing as a fighter is to become "more at peace within the storm" –

---

[2] *NAS Exhaustive Concordance of the Bible with Hebrew-Aramaic and Greek Dictionaries.* Copyright 1981, 1998 by the Lockman Foundation.
[3] Elbert Hubbard. (n.d.). BrainyQuote.com. Retrieved May 6, 2016, from BrainyQuote.com Website site: http://www.brainyquote.com/quotes/quotes/e/elberthubb3

the "storm" being the flurry of punches or kicks by an opponent! This helped me understand that the goal of the increased intensity and challenges in my training – once I had mastered the elementary skills – was to help me mature by testing my mental toughness to remain steady and disciplined. As the prophet Isaiah taught, *"You [Lord] will keep in perfect peace those who minds are steadfast, because they trust in you."* (Isaiah 26:3)

Once a fighter has mastered basic techniques and becomes comfortable with his skills, the intensity is increased, challenging the fighter to trust their technique rather than give into fear. The application of this lesson reminds me of Jesus' example in "calming the storm" as described in the Gospel of Matthew. It is one of my favorite passages in the Bible, because it was clearly set up by the Sovereign Lord to teach his disciples a lesson! After a long day of healing the sick, Jesus gave orders to cross to the other side of the lake.

> *Then he got into the boat and his disciples followed him. Suddenly a furious storm came up on the lake, so that the waves swept over the boat. But Jesus was sleeping. The disciples went and woke him, saying, "Lord, save us! We're going to drown!" He replied, "You of little faith, why are so afraid?" Then he got up and rebuked the winds and the waves, and it was completely calm. The men were amazed and asked, "What kind of man is this? Even the winds and the waves obey him!"* (Matthew 8:23-27)

I have often thought that Jesus was feigning sleep to see how his disciples would react, but since the Scriptures usually clarify that and did not do so in this instance, I surrendered to the fact that Jesus was genuinely asleep – at peace with the Father despite the crashing waves! His disciples, although experienced fishermen and sailors, were so scared that they frantically went to wake Jesus, thinking they were all going to drown! In the midst of the storm, Jesus rebuked them for their lack of faith in him and their fear of their circumstances. Only then did he stop the winds and waves, restoring the calm of the lake, leaving his disciples completely amazed. Their response was also telling, as they exposed their doubt in his divinity by stating, *"What kind of man is this?"* Their courage and conviction in Jesus as the Messiah had not yet fully solidified.

What do we learn from this? Our "fight of faith" will involve "storms" that are meant to test the integrity of our hearts. The result will either be to produce faith and trust in the power of God or fear and self-reliance that leads to our downfall. Jesus did not just have a typical storm appear on the lake – every fisherman is accustomed to storms – He allowed a *"furious"* storm to appear, one that was so frightening that even veteran fishermen gave in to fear for their lives! Even though Jesus was with them in the boat, they still gave into anxiety and fear. They had forgotten "who" was behind the storm!

In addition to highlighting the need to fight the "good fight of faith," the Book of Job also addresses the universal challenge to accept "unjust suffering." It is one thing to "battle" against an opponent with whom you stand a chance at winning; it is quite another to receive a "beat down" from an opponent because you have no answer to their attack! The tremendous physical pain which Job endured is simply this – a devastating "beat down" from the hands of Satan that became so infamous that it is known by pagans and the faithful alike. The deeper issue, however, is the depth of Job's emotional and spiritual predicament – issues that are often overlooked. However, we must not disregard these vital matters so that we will develop spiritual maturity and growth.

In Order To Effectively Examine The Book Of Job, This Book Is Divided Into 3 Major Parts:

1) THE COMPLEXITY OF THE COURT OF HEAVEN Job's Distress In The Face Of Personal Loss – The Challenge Of Physical Suffering (Ch. 1-3)

2) THE COMPLEXITY OF HUMANS Job's Defense At Being Misunderstood – The Challenge Of Emotional Suffering (Ch. 4-37)

3) THE COMPLEXITY OF HIS SOVEREIGNTY Job's Deliverance Despite His Bewilderment At God – The Challenge Of Spiritual Suffering (Ch. 38-42)

The Problem Of Suffering

Examining Job's journey through these three areas of "suffering" is an important case study for training every disciple of Jesus. Important truths about the nature of God, the agenda of Satan, and the character of men are made clear. One major issue that arises is God's toleration of Job's pain. While it is expected for flawed human beings – even friends – to hurt one another, it is usually uncomfortable for a Christian to accept the fact that an omnipotent and benevolent God would permit such horrific suffering: "If God is a just and competent 'referee,' why would he not protect a fighter who is no longer able to defend himself?" Extending this line of reasoning further, "Why should we entrust our souls into the hands of a supposedly 'indifferent' God, much less imperfect men?" Reconciling these challenges with God's perfect character continues to be a source of nagging questions for both the irreligious and faithful Christians, such as:

"If God is merciful, why does he watch innocent people suffer, such as victims of terrorism or a child with horrible and debilitating birth defects?"

"If God is good, why does he allow massive destruction and loss of life from the natural disasters of tornadoes, hurricanes and earthquakes?"

"If God is just, why does he permit man's inhumanity to man, such as the Jewish Holocaust and Rwandan Genocide?"

While there may be no immediate answers to these difficult questions, the Book of Job probes this "problem of suffering" with depth, honesty and profound insight that can only originate from the inspiration of God. Its importance is shared by the 19th century French poet and author Victor Hugo, who once stated, "Tomorrow if all literature was to be destroyed and it was left to me to retain one work only, I would save Job."[4]

Within this framework, the unknown writer of Job – under the inspiration of God's Spirit – provides us with one of Scripture's most penetrating and important works. Remarkably, this book of Holy Scripture stands alone amongst the books of the Old Testament with a form and theme that is unique. The Book of Job is the first of five books – Job, Psalms, Proverbs, Ecclesiastes and Song of Songs – commonly referred to as the "Books of Poetry" due to their poetic style in contrast to other narrative style of most other books. The Book of Job consists of diverse forms such as lament, wisdom sayings, proverbs, hymns, riddles, curses and lyrical nature poems. The evidence of its inspiration and historicity is confirmed by both the Old and New Testament quotes of Job in Ezekiel 14:14, 1 Corinthians 3:19, Romans 11:35, and James 5:11. As mentioned before, there is uncertainty in regards to who wrote it, or exactly when it was written, but the story appears to be set in the days of the patriarchs in the early third millennium BC.

---

[4] http://blueletterbible.org/study/eo/Job/Job000/cfm.

Job's long life (140 years), the measurement of his wealth in livestock, his functioning as a priest for his family, all fit the patriarchal period. It is not unreasonable to suppose that Job might have been a contemporary of Abraham, Issac or Jacob, whenever the Book of Job was given its final form. This view is perhaps supported by the Genesis 36:4 reference to an Eliphaz who was the first son of Esau and ancestor of the Edomites. The land where Job lived, Uz, is also associated with Edom (northern Arabia) in Lamentations 4:21.[5]

In addition to a synopsis of the Book of Job, one of the main goals of this book is to provide a helpful summary of the "do's and don'ts" in "giving and receiving" discipling in our lives. Many Christians do not take the time to examine the challenge of Job's "emotional pain," as he bears his heart to his three friends and tries to reconcile the will of God through their faulty counsel, and yet, the majority of the Book of Job is based on this challenge. (Job 4-37) It is my prayer that we can learn valuable lessons of counseling from the Book of Job, so we will be *competent to instruct one another.* (Romans 15:14)

As we begin this journey together in examining suffering in the Book of Job, take a moment to reflect on the following question: "How do I react to suffering in my life?" There are several responses that are present throughout this great book, yet only one is our faith proven genuine – to put our hope in the benevolent nature and ultimate sovereignty of God. (Job 42:1-3) As you contemplate your response, consider the five sinful responses:

Do you become faithless and curse God? (Job 2:9)

Do you become emotionally numb and give into self-pity? (Job 2:13)

---

[5] Reeve, James Josiah. *International Standard Bible Encyclopedia.*

Do you become anxious and fearful? (Job 3:25-26)

Do you believe you deserve the suffering because of your "guilty soul" or the opinions of others? (Job 4:8)

Do you condemn God's good judgment and discredit his word? (Job 40:8)

As a whole, the Book of Job is ageless and has a universal message. As we all gaze upon the magnificent cosmos of the heavens, we must recognize that we live with mystery – as the Apostle Paul states in Romans 11:33, *"Oh, the depths of the riches of the wisdom and knowledge of God! How unsearchable his judgments, and his paths beyond tracing out!"* It is impossible for us to completely explain "all that happens" to our world to a nation or to an individual, despite the wonders of God's revelation in Scripture and in Jesus Christ. Job reminds us of this reality and affirms the great truth that, despite our lack of knowledge, we can and must have faith. As a result, the Book of Job is one of the most important books in the Bible for disciples to explore. Each of us at times experiences suffering which we cannot explain. For times like these, a thorough study of Job offers insight and stimulates hope on how to overcome with faith and integrity, as we rely on God and each other, therefore being "proven genuine!"

PART 1: THE COMPLEXITY OF THE COURT OF HEAVEN

JOB'S DISTRESS THROUGH PERSONAL LOSS – THE CHALLENGE OF PHYSICAL SUFFERING

CHAPTER 1: THE TEST OF INTEGRITY

I don't trust a man who hasn't suffered... As diamonds are made by pressure and pearls formed by irritation, so greatness is forged by adversity. - John Eldredge, *Wild At Heart*[6]

With pressure exerted for millennia, worthless pieces of coal become precious diamonds!

Integrity In Personal And Family Leadership (Job 1:1-5)

In the opening prologue of Job, his character is described as *"...blameless and upright; he feared God and shunned evil... He was the greatest among all the people of the East."* (Job 1:1, 3b) Job is introduced as an upright man, who has been blessed with riches and a large family. It is significant that Job's abundant fortune had not produced arrogance toward a higher power beyond himself. By this time in his spiritual walk, Job had achieved a spiritual balance of being both prosperous and pious. It is possible to be both spiritual and wealthy! Job's example of godly integrity is unique, as financial prosperity can often lead to self-

---

[6] Eldredge, John (2001). *Wild At Heart: Discovering The Secret Of A Man's Soul.* Thomas Nelson Publishing.

satisfaction and pride towards God instead of humility and reliance on him. (Hosea 13:6) Job passes this test – unlike most people – and now he is ready for his next test! As Matthew Henry states in his concise commentary on Job, "By God's grace the temptations of worldly wealth can be overcome."[7] It is interesting to note that the tests of Job did not begin out of the physical challenges of poverty, but out of the spiritual temptations of prosperity!

An example of personal integrity in the area of finances that I admire is exemplified through my dear friends Michael and Sharon Kirchner. Michael refused a multi-million dollar compensation agreement and the vision to become the president of his division in the General Mills Company to *"seek first [God's] Kingdom"* and move his family from Minneapolis to Los Angeles to be part of a SoldOut Discipling Movement Church. (Matthew 6:33) Since that time, they have become a dearly loved source of inspiration and support, not only as a Shepherding Couple in the City of Angels International Christian Church, but all over the world as the World Sector Administrator Couple of our Movement! Out of their wealth accumulated from Michael's job at General Mills, the Kirchners have given hundreds of thousands of dollars to support the Movement's plan for forceful advancement into all the nations of the world. The Kirchners have heeded 1 Timothy 6:17-18, *"Command those who are rich in this present world not to be arrogant nor to put their hope in wealth, which is so uncertain, but to put their hope in God, who richly provides us with everything for our enjoyment. Command them to do good, to be rich in good deeds, and to be generous and willing to share."*

---

[7] Henry, Matthew (1706, 1991). *Matthew Henry's Concise Commentary.* Hendrickson Publishers.

Job's integrity shines through his humility, not only in his personal righteousness, but also in his care for his family. Like a true *"overseer,"* Job was intimately involved in leading the discipleship of his family's personal walk with God. (1 Timothy 3:1-5) Job 1:5 states, *"When a period of feasting had run its course, Job would send and have [his children] purified. Early in the morning he would sacrifice a burnt offering for each of them, thinking, 'Perhaps my children have sinned and cursed God in their hearts.' This was Job's regular custom."* Job's priest-like actions to care for his family indicates his concern for discipling their hearts to honor God, reminding us of the admonition from the writer of Hebrews, *"See to it, brothers and sisters, that none of you has a sinful, unbelieving heart that turns away from the living God."* (Hebrews 3:12) Psalm 50:23 reads, *"He who sacrifices thank offerings honors me, and he prepares the way so that I may show him the salvation of God."* Job's heart to honor God also served to prepare the way for his family to be saved!

How does Job's example of integrity, both personally and for his family, relate to you? Very often the security of wealth tends to make us complacent in our spiritual walk. We focus more on getting to work on time than getting to church on time; we focus more on our financial portfolios than our spiritual profiles. Sadly, we can become so self-consumed due to our love for wealth that we are *"never satisfied with our income."* (Ecclesiastes 5:10) As a result, our time is monopolized more and more by the increase of financial wealth rather than serving to make others spiritually "wealthy" by investing in the Lord! (2 Corinthians 6:10) To be clear, obtaining wealth and possessions and the ability to enjoy them is *"a gift of God."* (Ecclesiastes 5:19) However, we must also remember the admonition of Solomon – the wealthiest man of all time – as stated in Ecclesiastes 5:15, *"Naked a man comes from his mother's womb, and as he comes, so he departs. He takes nothing from his labor that he can carry in his hand."* Let us all imitate Job's heart for God and for leading his family by honoring the Great Commandments given to us by the Lord, *"Love the Lord your God with all your heart and with all your soul and with all your mind... and love your neighbor as yourself!"* (Matthew 22:37-39)

Integrity In Motives (Job 1:6-12)

In this passage, we have the privilege to understand the context of Job's testing by getting a "behind the scenes" glimpse of the Royal Court of Heaven – multitudes of subjects that have assembled before the throne of God, bowing before him in complete reverence with the freedom to make humble requests. The *"Accuser"* of mankind – Satan – who *"masquerades as an angel of light"* is also present, having been *"roaming through the earth and going back and forth in it."* (Job 1:7b; 2 Corinthians 11:14) The dramatic events of these opening chapters – of which Job is completely unaware – is God's admonition for Satan to acknowledge Job's integrity and righteous example.

> *Then the Lord said to Satan, "Have you considered my servant Job? There is no one on Earth like him; he is blameless and upright, a man who fears God and shuns evil."*
>
> *"Does Job fear God for nothing?" Satan replied. "Have you not put a hedge around him and his household and everything he has? You have blessed the work of his hands... But now stretch out your hand and strike everything he has, and he will surely curse you to your face."* (Job 1:8-11)

This passage makes it clear that God is the actual initiator behind Job's test. Yet while Satan uses and discards human beings in a casual and cruel manner, God does not.

Therefore, the reasons for Job's suffering are found in God's character and purposes rather than in Satan's. Satan's response to God is more of a sneering retort, accusing Job of having selfish motives for his piety. He claims that Job is simply worshipping God out of a selfish ambition to keep his prosperity, not out of genuine devotion. Sadly, this accusation has been clearly shown to have merit in the religious world of today, as the teaching of a "prosperity gospel" sees God as more of a "genie" to be flattered for a reward than a God to be worshiped for his love. Satan is clearly challenging the integrity of Job's worship of God, asserting that God is not worthy of praise on the basis of his nature alone. This is an assault not only on the character of Job, but on mankind as a whole. As Psalm 96:4-6 proclaims, *"For great is the Lord and most worthy of praise; he is to be feared above all gods. For all the gods of the nations are idols, but the Lord made the heavens. Splendor and majesty are before him; strength and glory are in his sanctuary."*

What are your motives for pleasing God? Do you believe that God is worthy of praise on the basis of his nature alone? This is a very important issue for those who struggle with keeping a heart of "desire" for the will of God rather than a heart of "duty." As Proverbs 16:2 teaches, *"All a man's ways seem innocent to him, but motives are weighed by the Lord."* Satan's argument, though clearly malicious, is accurate of human nature. Our motives are often impure and selfish. Even the motives of our prayers can be the result of a heart to *"spend what (we) get on (our) pleasures"* rather than to glorify God. (James 4:3)

Consider the following questions: Why do you pray for a more prestigious job? To have a greater influence to save souls or just for more money? Why do you attend church services? To worship God and love others, or for God to

41

bless your life and be persuaded that you do not deserve to be punished? Why do you read your Bible? As an academic pursuit of knowledge or to grow deeper in your faith and love for the grace and mercy of God? Very often we are tempted to forget his benefits and lose our gratitude! (Psalm 103:1-5) It is at this time that we become more religious than righteous, and our relationship with God becomes more of a ritual than a relationship.

What is the answer? We must heed the Apostle Paul's admonition in 2 Corinthians 13:5, *"Examine yourselves to see whether you are in the faith; test yourselves."* We must put our motives under the microscope of God's word and the examination of other Christians so that we are not *"hardened by sin's deceitfulness."* (Hebrews 3:12-13) We might just find that we fear God not because of his power, but because we fear the loss of his provisions! Job's purity of heart caused God to take notice.

> *Who may ascend the hill of the Lord? Who may stand in his holy place? He who has clean hands and a pure heart, who does not lift up his soul to an idol or swear by what is false. He will receive blessing from the Lord and vindication from God his Savior.* (Psalm 24:3-5)

This Scripture should inspire us all, as the purity of Job's motives was so impactful that they reached the attention of the throne room of Heaven! However, it is challenging to note that the blessing and vindication from the Lord would not be made clear until Job endured much suffering.

Integrity And Misfortune: Family And Finances (1:13-22)

10 children... 10 graves. Any parent only has to imagine what this would be like to immediately have compassion on Job and his wife for such a horrific tragedy. As Job has no awareness of the heavenly scene which has been drawn out

for us, Satan has clearly organized the timing of the devastating losses experienced by Job to suggest divine intervention. Satan's goal is clear – to use misfortune as an opportunity to blame God. Likewise, we must also be careful not to blame God for unexpected and awful events. (Job 1:13-19) We have no access to the information we need to judge the ultimate purposes of God.

Job's grief is probably not relegated solely to his now bankrupt status, although this is a typical "domino effect" of suffering that is often used by Satan to weaken one's integrity. In the movie *Saving Private Ryan* (1998), the American Army sent out a squad of soldiers with the sole purpose of rescuing the last missing son of a grief-stricken mother who had already lost three sons in battle. Similarly, we can only imagine the compassion of God as he watched the anguish of Job and his wife, with their only solace being that of knowing that Job's children would rest with the Lord. Despite this unthinkable loss of his 10 children and all of his wealth, Job simply falls to the ground in worship. The key Scripture of this chapter is Job 1:21-22, *"'Naked I came from my mother's womb, and naked I will depart. The Lord gave and the Lord has taken away, may the name of the Lord be praised.' In all this, Job did not sin by charging God with wrongdoing."* Job's example of worship should be our goal – to honor God as Sovereign and trust his will to direct our lives.

The integrity of Job through misfortune is displayed by his decision to not give into the entitlement that easily accompanies the accumulation of possessions. Family and wealth are not a right, but a privilege and gift from God. Consider the words of Solomon in Ecclesiastes 5:19, *"Moreover, when God gives someone wealth and possessions, and the ability to enjoy them, to accept their lot and be happy in their toil – this is a gift of God."*

The seeds of bitterness towards God can easily develop when we believe that what we deserve is not given to us – which leads to the sin of "acedia" – defined as "a state of restlessness and inability either to work or to pray," a "worldly sorrow" that is a "willful refusal to enjoy the goodness of God and the world God created."[8] Job's righteous example despite his ignorance of Satan's vindictive challenge to God proves the genuine nature of his faith and the strength of his endurance and integrity. This was remarkable given that from Job's perspective, there was no assurance of a future life. For Job, death was the end, so justice would have to occur in this life. Although Satan had predicted he would make Job curse God, neither the anguish caused by Job's loss of wealth and family or the agony caused by his illness embittered Job to ***"sin by charging God with wrongdoing."*** (Job 1:22) Satan, who had set the conditions of this contest, lost. We can only imagine what was going on in Job's heart and mind through this time – the thoughts and feelings that surged through him as the proposed "evidence" mounted that the God he served had turned against him.

As I reflect on my personal life, I can sympathize with Job as I consider the pain that I endured from the loss of family to tragedy. In August 2008, I endured the death of my mother to cancer and wrestled with the pain associated with her untimely loss. Even as I write these words I cannot do so without tears. My mother was an incredible example of hard work, love and loyalty to her family. I still recall her servant heart as she got up early in the morning during one of my visits home to make me breakfast – in a severely weakened state. Her death was one of the most challenging times in my Christian walk, and I felt a strong temptation to be bitter at God; bitter at the false doctrine that she adhered to; bitter at

---

[8] McKean, Dr. Thomas. *Acedia: The Forgotten Sin.* Retrieved from www.caicc.net. June 16, 2014

her stubbornness to accept the clear truth that she acknowledged; bitter at the fact that a loving woman who cared for others as a nurse could not be spared the agony of a painful death.

The author's mother, Eila Smellie, as she battled Stage 4 colon cancer.

I found solace in the knowledge that the Lord had blessed me with seven years to shower my mother with love rather than endure her sudden loss by a heart attack or stroke. It was Job's tearful admonition in Job 1:21 that softened my heart and helped me to overcome the pain. I was reminded that God's gift of my mother was not something I deserved. I needed to handle my grief in a godly way by not feeling entitled to the time that I had with her. When God takes a loved one away, be grateful – you never deserved the relationship in the first place.

As the Lord saw fit, my mother died on August 28, 2008 and her funeral was scheduled for September 7th, although preparations had already been made for me to plant and lead the Inaugural Service of the Washington DC International Christian Church on September 14th. The rigors of leading a church planting and conducting the Inaugural Service seven days after my mother's funeral were daunting. Yet I understood this was my duty as an Evangelist in the Kingdom of God. As Jesus stated in Luke 9:59-60 (AMP), *"And he said to another, 'Become my disciple, side with my party, and accompany me!' But he replied, 'Lord, permit me first to go and bury (await the death of) my father.' But Jesus said to him, 'Allow the dead to bury their own dead; but as for you, go and spread the news of the kingdom of God.'"*

While Jesus' response may seem callous to the casual reader, his perfect will is clear. Funerals are not for the dead; they are for the living. The spiritually dead can bury the physically dead, but those who are spiritually alive need to use their time to proclaim the kingdom. All my efforts to encourage my mother to accept the truth over my time as a disciple – eight years at that point – had come to an end. No more could be done, except to move the hearts of those who loved her to seek the truth. At her funeral, I shared a eulogy from Psalm 90:12 to encourage those in attendance to ask God to *"teach us to number our days, so that we may gain a heart of wisdom."* After playing one of her favorite piano pieces – "Consolation No. 3" by Franz Liszt, I touched her casket and comforted our family at her gravesite. Then my wife and I drove 280 miles back to Washington DC to prepare for our Inaugural Service on the following Sunday. With just 16 disciples the Lord blessed us with 134 in attendance, a glorious baptism, a moving restoration and two disciples who placed membership! About 15 months later, the Spirit had grown the mission team of 16 to 47 sold-out disciples! My

46

heart was comforted as the integrity of my decision to not give into sentimentality was proven genuine. Although I had to wrestle with the fact that I did not "know" God's purposes behind my mother's death, I chose to remain faithful.

Do you have to "know" the reasons behind God's purposes to obey his will? Are you easily moved by the emotional pull of family and friends to turn your back on God and his mission? Do not allow your lack of understanding of God's purposes shake your faith in his constant love.

CHAPTER 2: THE TEST OF ENDURANCE

All through my life, I have been tested. My will has been tested, my courage has been tested, my strength has been tested. Now my patience and endurance are being tested. [9] - Muhammed Ali during his struggle with Parkinson's Disease

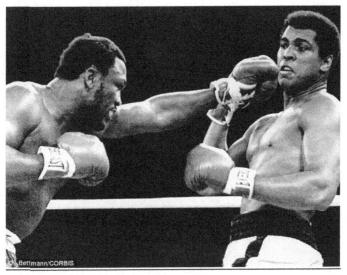

Mohammed Ali (right) fighting Joe Frazier in 1973!

Endurance Is Honored By God (Job 2:1-6)

It is challenging enough to go through a horrific event in one day – but then the nightmare continues… The Lord again puts Job's integrity and endurance on display before Satan with an added emphasis in Job 2:3, ***"And he still maintains his integrity, though you incited me against him to ruin him without any reason."*** Satan had declared that Job's

---

[9] Ali, Muhammed (2004). *The Soul of a Butterfly: Reflections on Life's Journey.* Simon & Schuster.

integrity had no foundation, and it would be easily overcome and dissipate. The Lord was confident in Job's faithfulness and allowed Satan to attack it. Following, God declared Job's integrity with his own mouth. Job's integrity had not been wrestled from him; he still maintained it. The Hebrew of the above verse means to literally "swallow him up;" i.e. "to ruin him, overwhelm him with calamities when he had done nothing to deserve such treatment." [10] Since God is sovereign, everything that happened to Job was either allowed to happen or made to happen by God. This Scripture proves that God is neither sadistic or lacking in compassion, but rather a being of principle and integrity himself. (Hebrews 6:18)

In our generation, the word integrity is characterized as having a noble character behind closed doors as well as in the public light. Our understanding grows deeper, however, when we understand that the word integrity is related to the word integrate. In *The Book of Manliness*, author Stephen Mansfield describes how the Latin word integras – which means "soundness, wholeness or entire" – was used in the Roman ritual to inspect the integrity of its soldiers:

The army of ancient Rome used this word (integrity) almost daily in its inspection ritual. A commander would walk through the line of legionaries, inspecting each man to confirm that he was fit for duty. As the commander came before one of his men, the soldier would sweep his fist hard in to the middle of his chest, just over his heart, and shout "Integras!" The commander first listened for that rich, full quality of a healthy soldier's voice and then he listened for the clang that well-kept armor would emit when struck. The two

---

[10] http://biblehub.com/commentaries/job/2-3.htm. *Barnes' Notes on the Bible*

sounds – the man's voice and the condition of his armor – confirmed the integrity of the soldier.[11]

The word indicates soundness through and through. This characterizes the character of Job. Integrity, exposed through endurance, confirms the training that is beneath the surface. One of the most inspiring examples of endurance and integrity for Patrique and me are our dear friends and mentors, Kip & Elena McKean. Despite the betrayal of friends, the falling away of their children, and the destruction of our former fellowship, their desire to ***"(fight) the good fight"*** of faith has once again led them to become the visionary leaders for God's New Movement! (2 Timothy 4:7) Their convictions have been proven genuine through their trials, and their faith has come forth as gold!

The author and his wife with the McKeans at the Portland World Missions Jubilee in 2004!

---

[11] Mansfield, Stephen (2013). *Manfield's Book of Manly Men: An Utterly Invigorating Guide to Being Your Most Masculine Self.* Nelson Books. Page 161.

In The Hands Of Satan (Job 2:7-10)

Before Job's first set of tests, the Lord said to Satan, *"Everything he has is in your hands, but on the man himself do not lay a finger."* (Job 1:12) Now in Job's second set of tests, the Lord said to Satan, *"He is in your hands; but you must spare his life."* (Job 2:6)

For me, I found Job extraordinary to be surrendered in the face of catastrophes that eliminated his wealth, and even more so, caused the loss of all of his children. Now with the threat to Job's personal health, the difficulty to stay righteous became even more challenging – and God allowed it to happen to prove Job's integrity.

What was the challenge to his health? The brief description in Job 2:8 suggests boils, ulcers or some other painful skin disease that caused acute suffering. Other references in Job develop a picture of disfigurement and anguish. Job was subject to sores and/or boils (Job 2:7), itching (Job 2:8), drastic changes in appearance (Job 2:12), sleeplessness (Job 7:4), worms and running sores (Job 7:5), depression (Job 7:16, 30:15), dimmed eyesight (Job 16:16), putrid breath (Job 19:17), rotting teeth (Job 19:20), emaciation (Job 19:20), corroding bones and pain (Job 30:17), and blacked skin and exhausting fevers (Job 30:30) for months (Job 7:3, 29:2). His suffering was so intense and obvious that when his friends saw him they had nothing to say. (Job 2:11-13)

For many disciples, the heart of integrity is often honed over time, and if they are able to "pass the test" of impure motives or misfortune, they are definitely weakened by the attack of ill health. The vision and development of the Lazarus Ministry by Kip McKean during his leadership of the Portland Church was inspirational in meeting this need. This incredible group of disciples persevered in their faith and encouraged others to remain strong despite the challenges of chronic and in some cases even terminal illnesses. Their theme Scripture was Romans 5:3-5, *"Not only so, but we also glory in our sufferings, because we know that suffering produces perseverance; perseverance, character; and character, hope. And hope does not put us to shame, because God's love has been poured out into our hearts through the Holy Spirit, who has been given to us."*

What is so remarkable about the character of Job is that he had no knowledge of the power of the Holy Spirit. That said, he continued to hope with no evidence of entitlement in his heart. At this point, Job's integrity has been put on display by God, tested by Satan, and then even questioned by his wife. After experiencing both the loss of security in wealth and enduring funerals for the 10 children that she bore, Job's wife said to him, "Are you still maintaining your integrity? Curse God and die!" Perhaps she thought that death was preferable to life, and the cursing of God by Job would lead to a swift end to his suffering by the punishment of God. Despite her reaction, Job patiently challenged his wife to resist the temptation of self-pity and hopelessness that is so easily associated with heartache and discouragement.

On a personal note, I thank God for blessing me with a wife who has endured much yet remained faithful in her walk with God. Despite challenges with anemia and acid-reflux that developed during her law school studies, as well as diabetes and sciatica that developed from her pregnancies, Patrique has continued to have a powerful faith and trust in God. Even when the doctors believed our first child would actually be a miscarriage, she never gave up hope. She has been an incredible example of faith in our Sovereign God!

The author's courageous family – Patrique, Isaiah & Naomi – before planting the Lagos Church in 2016!

A Few Loyal Friends (Job 2:11-13)

Imagine… the news goes out about the loss of your entire family; you become bankrupt; and are afflicted with horrendous health challenges, yet only three of your hundreds of "Facebook friends" even bother to come and see you. How would you feel? Job's experience here reminds me of when Jesus was seized and led away to be maliciously tried and tortured for false crimes, and only *"Peter [and John] followed at a distance."* (Luke 22:54; John 18:15) True friendships are shown at times of challenge and heartbreak. Considering that all three of Job's friends lived significant distances away, it is noteworthy to see the effort they made to communicate with one another and plan their visit together. Given all the calamities, it probably was some months before the news of Job's misfortunes reached them. (Job 7:3)

There are only two possible references to Eliphez the Temanite outside of the Book of Job that might help us ascertain his identity. There was an Eliphaz, the son of Esau by his wife Adah (Genesis 36:4), but he most likely is not the person mentioned in Job. However, the Temanites were celebrated for their wisdom as we learn from Jeremiah 49:7,

53

and this reference also makes implications to Esau and Edom. To be noted, neither Bildad the Shuhite or Zophar the Naamathite are mentioned anywhere else in Scripture, nor is there any mention of the Shuhites or Naamatites.

Seeing a disfigured Job from a distance, sitting *"among the ashes"* must have been too much for these three friends to bear as they began to weep aloud. (Job 2:8) Romans 12:15 reminds us all to *"mourn with those who mourn,"* and they sat with him for a considerable amount of time in silence without saying a word. The period of *"seven days"* was an appropriate time of mourning. (Genesis 1:10) The long silence may be accounted for by the fact that "among the Jews," "it is a point of decorum, and one dictated by a fine and true feeling, not to speak to a person in deep affliction until he gives an intimation of a desire to be comforted."[12] So long as Job kept silent, they were silent. They could probably speak to attendants who brought them food or to each other, but *"no one said a word to him."* (Job 2:13)

As chapter two comes to a close, some would suggest that this "divine wager" which is often categorized as a contest between God and Satan – with Job as a pawn – has proven Job's integrity, as Satan is defeated by Job's example and is not mentioned again in the book. Remarkably, Job's suffering continues! It is clear that God has a purpose beyond victory in this supposed "contest" with Satan. In order to guard our hearts from misunderstanding or bitterness regarding the will of God, we must also seek comfort in the knowledge that God has a purpose in mind during our trials – with the goal for our faith to be proven genuine!

---

[12] http://biblehub.com/commentaries/job/2-13.htm (*Pulpit Commentary*, verse 13 – reference by Cook)

CHAPTER 3: TRUSTING OUR ULTIMATE "REFEREE"

"Trust in him at all times, you people; pour out your hearts to him, for God is our refuge." - King David in Psalm 62:8

Job as portrayed in the haunting painting
by Léon Bonnat.

A Blessing Or A Curse? (Job 3:1-10)

After being silent for over a week with his friends nearby, Job finally speaks and curses the day of his birth. (Job 3:3) He is filled with a despondency that is honest as he struggles to understand God's purpose behind his sufferings. He has now come to the point where his discouraged wife had come to earlier – *"Curse God and die!"* (Job 2:9) – yet he does not sin by cursing God, but only hopes to die. Job has become weary, tired and has gone the distance of his perceived endurance. His words resemble the heartache of the prophet Jeremiah, who also experienced much suffering. (Jeremiah 20:14-18) It is important to note that despite Job's agony, he never contemplates suicide outright, but perhaps gave into passive suicidal thoughts. (Job 3:11) The act of suicide would be sin, as it would destroy the temple of God. (1 Corinthians 3:17) It is clear here that Job's outcry is more than just the challenges of his ill health, but one of a broken spirit. As Proverbs 18:14 states, *"The human spirit can endure in sickness, but a crushed spirit who can bear?"*

Many have experienced that which typically troubles disciples the most in their sufferings, not the physical pain, but the mental anguish. Job cannot understand the "why" of his experience, which has shaken his most cherished beliefs in God. One of the great values of the Book of Job is that it teaches us not to hide our emotions. There are many who would be critical of Job – as we will soon discover from his three friends – for expressing his anguish so strongly. Yet it is Job's honesty in expressing his feelings that reminds us that God understands our feelings and accepts them as we work through our times of suffering to a deeper, more perfect faith. Consider the words of Jesus as worked through his heart to accept the cross in the Garden of Gethsemane:

> *Then Jesus went with his disciples to a place called Gethsemane, and he said to them, "Sit*

56

here while I go over there and pray." *He took* *Peter and the two sons of Zebedee along with* *him, and he began to be sorrowful and troubled.* *Then he said to them, "My soul is overwhelmed* *with sorrow to the point of death.* *Stay here and* *keep watch with me."* (Matthew 26:36-38) Jesus' heart to be honest about his emotions with God and men is an important connection to Job. The testing of our faith and our trust in the righteous sovereignty of God can become a mountain to climb when it appears that God's plan to make us holy may also include "harming us" through life's twists and turns – or even through the well-intentioned but hurtful actions of family, friends or fellow Christians! The faithful have often taken comfort in their trials by remembering the Lord's encouragement to the Jewish exiles in Babylonian captivity as presented by the prophet Jeremiah, *"'For I know the plans I have for you,' declares the Lord,* *'plans to prosper you and not to harm you, plans to give* *you hope and a future.'"* (Jeremiah 29:11) Despite this promise from God, our own perspective in dealing with the "problem of pain" in our lives can be troubling. If we are to apply this Scripture to the plight of all righteous men and women of God, how are we to explain the unwarranted suffering of martyrs? Could the *"harm"* that the Lord speaks of be related to the "final destiny" of punishment for every wicked and unrepentant human being? (Psalm 73:17) If so, then what is the purpose of our hardship while here on Earth? Are God's plans harmful or helpful?

This question leads many to challenge God's integrity in order to justify their own. As Hebrews 12:7,11 states, *"Endure* *hardship as discipline... No discipline seems pleasant at* *the time, but painful. Later on, however, it produces a* *harvest of righteousness and peace for those who have* *been trained by it."* As a soldier is trained to remain disciplined during the heat of battle, it is the challenge of every

Christian to submit to the wisdom of God's *"painful"* training: Being made holy through hardship so we may be at *"peace"* during the attacks of Satan. This training through life's challenges endures so that we can produce a *"harvest of righteousness"* in our character instead of the lukewarmness that develops from a lack of maturity. Hebrews 12:7-11 makes it clear that what appears to be *"harm"* from God to those lacking spiritual understanding is actually *"for our good."* (Hebrews 12:10) Sadly, those who lack the humility to acknowledge this Biblical truth end up questioning God's love and sovereignty and begin to justify their own bitterness. The prophet Isaiah reminds us of the comfort that God desires to provide for his people during their trials.

> *Why do you say, O Jacob, and complain, O Israel, "My way is hidden from the Lord; my cause is disregarded by my God?" Do you not know? Have you not heard? The Lord is the everlasting God, the Creator of the ends of the Earth. He will not grow tired or weary, and his understanding no one can fathom. He gives strength to the weary and increases the power of the weak. Even youths grow tired and weary, and young men stumble and fall; but those who hope in the Lord will renew their strength. They will soar on wings like eagles; they will run and not grow weary, they will walk and not be faint.* (Isaiah 40:27-31)

Job is struggling to realize that he cannot fathom God's understanding, and he has yet to envision the development of increased strength and power that he will obtain if he overcomes. Like athletes at the brink of physical and emotional failure, Job (and disciples alike) can either give into self-pity or exercise self-discipline. All the while God is silent. He gives no answer for Job's trials. Job is struggling to see the final outcome. As the Scriptures state in Proverbs 29:18, *"Where there is no revelation, people cast off restraint; but blessed is the one who heeds wisdom's instruction."*

Sadly, Job has finally lost his restraint. He has lost vision for what God is doing, and therefore believes that he must perish. His joy is gone because he has not received any instruction or answer from the Lord. As he struggles with his circumstances, Job begins a liturgy of questions that reveal the depth of his despair.

When Doubts Challenge Truth (Job 3:11-26)

The "questioning phase" of faith is always the most unsteady time for a man or a woman of God. A common moniker of the "Phases of Faith" goes simply like this: Phase 1 – Chaos (non-Christian days); Phase 2 – Conformity (a "baby Christian" learning); Phase 3 – Questioning (a Christian facing doubts); Phase 4 – Conviction (a Christian that has overcome and prevailed). Such is the state of Job. Like any emotional teenager who knows what is good, yet does not understand its significance, Job's trials have brought him to a state of emotional uncertainty leading him to question everything. The danger of this phase is that feelings can become truth. Since Job wants to be at peace, and believes that only death can bring it, he utters in despair, *"For now I would be lying down in peace; I would be at asleep and at rest with kings and counselors of the Earth, who built for themselves places now lying in ruins."* (Job 3:13-14) What is the implication of this passage? Is it that the kings and counselors of the Earth, who do not know God, are at peace in death? Of course, this is false, but it is due to Job yielding to his "pains" that has now brought uncertainty to his former convictions. (Job 3:25)

How does this relate to a disciple? Simply put, a fragile emotional state can make us question Biblical truths. This

59

becomes a reality when Christians start to struggle in their faith and question clear Biblical truths due to a death of a loved one in their family; they now begin to doubt their loved one's spiritual state because the pain of acknowledging their physical and spiritual loss is too much to bear. Yet the Scriptures remind us in Proverbs 23:23 to *"buy the truth and do not sell it; get wisdom, discipline and understanding."* We cannot "sell-out" the truth to placate our feelings. We must heed the words of Jesus in John 8:31, *"If you hold to my teaching, you are really my disciples. Then you will know the truth, and the truth will set you free."*

The problem of suffering is a problem for us all, yet we must not waver. It is when the trials of life come that we remember the promises of God. As Romans 4:20 declares about the faith of Abraham, *"Yet he did not waver through unbelief regarding the promise of God, but was strengthened in his faith and gave glory to God, being fully persuaded that God had power to do what he had promised."* Faith, not fear, must be our defense in the midst of hopelessness and despair. Discipline, not doubt, must be the goal of our training to prepare us for these moments that will come.

In Job's situation, his question of "why" is one of the unanswerable questions that makes our trust in God an act of faith. (Job 3:20-25) Why God gives life and yet permits some who receive that gift to experience misery is answered in part later in the Book of Job. But often the "why" God permits us to suffer is not answered in this life. The difference between Jesus' honesty in expressing his emotions and Job's example is revealed in his statement, *"What I feared has come upon me; what I dreaded has happened to me."* (Job 3:25) This verse may be the key to the reason God permitted Job's suffering. Job feared God and tried to serve him, yet he also feared the future. Through this experience,

Job found a deeper faith, one that would free him from the terror of the future and permit a deeper love and trust for God.

A negative consequence of the fear and doubt that can arise as one deals with the emotional pain of suffering is the contempt of God and/or man – specifically those in leadership. (Deuteronomy 17:12-13) In over 15 years of ministry experience, I have dealt first-hand with different situations of contemptuous disciples who were deceived by Satan to give into their doubts and fears and leave the church... and thus God! It usually starts from discontent, then disagreement, and finally ends in outright contempt. The Merriam-Webster dictionary defines "contempt" as: "the act of despising – the state of mind of one who despises; to lack respect or reverence for something."[13] Many, if not all, were once powerful disciples who took valiant stands for the truth in the face of persecution. Yet, when the physical challenges of sacrificial giving or the emotional challenges of friends leaving or spiritual expectations were not achieved, they became unfulfilled and grew bitter. Instead of trusting in the sovereignty of God and "bearing up" under their perceived challenges, they believed the lie of Satan that the church was causing them "unjust suffering" and not looking out for their best interests. The Apostle Peter wrote an interesting perspective in regards to this:

For it is commendable if someone bears up under the pain of unjust suffering because they are conscious of God. But how is it to your credit if you receive a beating for doing wrong and endure it? But if you suffer for doing good and you endure it, this is commendable before God. To this you were called, because Christ suffered

---

[13] http://merriam-webster.com/dictionary/contempt

for you, leaving you an example, that you should follow in his steps. (1 Peter 2:19-21)

Instead of pouring out their hearts to God until they reached a point of surrender, they refused to believe the truth and started pouring out their hearts in dissension to other disciples – poisoning them with the seeds of doubt and mistrust. The Book of Acts also records a similar situation in Acts 14:2, *"But the Jews who refused to believe stirred up the other Gentiles and poisoned their minds against the brothers."*

What is the answer to this lack of trust and discontent? Get honest and open about your bitterness and get help – no matter whether you are at fault or not. Go to the person and seek to reconcile and understand their position. Even if you are unsuccessful in helping them to understand your perspective, you would have at least won a victory in understanding theirs. Ultimately, even if they are in sin, imitate the heart of Jesus and protect your heart. As Jesus stated, *"Father, forgive them, for they do not know what they are doing."* (Luke 23:34) The Apostle Paul also offers some key advice:

Brothers and sisters, if someone is caught in a sin, you who live by the Spirit should restore that person gently. But watch yourselves or you also may be tempted... If anyone thinks they are something when they are not, they deceive themselves. Each one should test their own actions. (Galatians 6:1,3-4a)

It is this temptation that causes people to give into contempt. They believe that because their antagonist is "in sin," they are justified in being unrighteous. As result, they fall into the Devil's trap of bitterness and into the sin of contempt. And then "unrighteous sparring" begins…

TESTIMONIAL: SEYI AKIN-AJAYI

My name is Seyi Akin-Ajayi, a recent graduate of the University of Lagos and baptized as a disciple of Jesus Christ in 2017. On November 4, 2018, I was kicked out of the house by my dad for going to church when he had instructed me not to go to "that church" anymore referring to the Lagos International Christian Church. Earlier on Sunday, October 28, 2018, I went to church as usual and when I came back I met my family at home. That evening, while I was in the living room with my mum and brother, my dad asked me where I went today and I told him I went to church. He asked me which church and I told him the church I usually attend at university. He became very angry and asked why I did not tell him before I went out to church. Our custom was to always inform our dad about where we were going, but that Sunday he was not in the house so there was no way I could inform him. He began yelling at me that I did not inform him, and when my dad gets angry, it is better not to say anything because that would make it worse. So, I kept quiet.

He began to talk about how he did not send me to college to go and join a church. He complained that the church is too far and that if I had been in an accident while going to church, I would have just wasted my life. He talked to me about me waking up in the morning and reading the Bible, saying it was being used to brainwash me instead of looking for how I can make my life better. He insulted me and called me so many names. As well, he threatened to curse me, while accusing me of placing religion above family and school. He went on to say that if I am not going to listen to him, then I can leave the house and kill myself and he would not even mourn me. He also insulted my mum saying that she cannot control me.

Throughout that week, he did not give me money. He usually gives my brother and me money for food everyday, because as students we were not cooking any food in the house. He warned me never to go to "that church" again. So it was not until Friday that my father spoke to me. To my shame, I had made up my mind not to go to church, because of his threats. I wanted to stay out of trouble and avoid conflict with my father, so I told my discipler on Saturday night that I was not coming to church. I also informed the campus minister, Tolani, about the whole situation and that I would not be coming to church. My discipler challenged me to still come out to church. After considering it and praying, I decided to write a letter to my dad explaining that I respect him and have always obeyed everything he told me to do but that when it comes to my faith as a Christian, I have to follow what the Bible says. Hence, I cannot obey his instructions not to go to church, but I can obey every other thing he tells me. I also explained why I could not go to other churches. I did not go into details about this because my dad does not believe in the Bible, Jesus or Christianity.

After writing the letter that night, I prayed and knocked on his door informing him I wanted to give him something. He asked me to put it on his table and I did. I was expecting he would read it that day but he did not. On Sunday morning, I was very scared and waiting to see how he would react, but he still had not read the letter. There was a meeting in our community where we live, because thieves had been coming around frequently so my dad was not at home as he attended the meeting. I summoned some courage and asked a brother, Bode, to send me some money, as I did not have any money for transport. I wanted to inform my dad before I left, but he was not in the house so I decided to call his phone, but he had left it at home. I called my mum, but she was not picking up. So, I sent both of them a message that I was going to church and then I left. While on my way, I received a call from my mum asking me where I was. I told her I was on my way to church. She responded to this by saying that if I do not come back immediately, I should not come back to the house again. My dad collected the phone from her and said the same thing then he hung up. My siblings were calling me, but I did not answer the phone.

So I arrived at church that day and I was very scared because I did not know what I was going back to face at home. After the church service, I boarded a bus back home with another disciple (Mofe), because she was also taking the same route with me. I told her about what happened, and how my dad might kick me out of the house and even physically assault me. My plan – which I told her about – was to leave the house and make my way to the brothers' household if that happened. However, I mentioned that I did not have any money for that. So before we stepped off the bus, she put something into my bag, and when I checked it was 1,000 naira (approximately $3)! Honestly, I felt embarrassed at first, but I knew I needed the money in case things got ugly. So I expressed my gratitude and ensured that she boarded another bus before I jumped on to a direct bus to home. I remember praying throughout the ride home.

When I arrived home, I saw my dad sitting outside with an angry look on his face. As I was about to enter the house, he asked me, "What are you doing?" I replied, "I want to come in." I went in and my dad also came in to meet me in the room, and he shouted, "I told you not to go to that church, but you went, right?" And he asked me if I have another place to sleep, but I did not answer. He left the room and came back again. This time, he acted surprised to see me and he asked, "Are you still in this house? I give you five minutes to pack your things and leave." So I started packing, but before I could pack much, he came in again and shouted in anger all the louder that he does not want me to have anything. He asked me to get out of the house, and just before he finished the sentence, he threw a punch and started raining punches on me. Then my mum and elder sister tried to hold him, but he was so violent that they could not hold him back. When he was done with the punches, he took my phone and my laptop. Then he searched me to see if there was any money, as his plan was to get me stranded, but I had hidden the money. I turned to go outside and immediately my dad turned around and attempted to use the laptop to hit me in the face, but I was able to parry it. At this point, he mentioned that he had disowned me.

Seyi (right) with his son in the faith, Daniel!

I went out immediately and he met me outside. This time with a huge stick and he said he was going to "make me bleed" before I go. My mum and sister were in the way, and I figured that there was no way to escape without someone getting injured. My elder sister was already crying and trying to beg my dad to stop. So while he was not looking, I scaled the fence into my neighbor's house; then scaled another fence into the second neighbor's house, and surprisingly their gate was opened, so I quickly made my way to safety. Shaken but actually stronger in my faith, I boarded a bus to the brothers' household. I have been staying there ever since. Sadly, I have yet to speak with my dad. It is important to know that my mum is not with my dad on this. In fact, she understands me pretty well. She had to act as if she was supporting him in order to avoid more issues. I have been in touch with my mum and siblings ever since the incident. Please pray for me to safely reconcile with my dad if possible, and perhaps someday baptize my mum, my siblings and… my dad! (Romans 12:18) I trust that God is in control.

PART 2: THE COMPLEXITY OF HUMANS

JOB'S DISTRESS THROUGH BEING MISUNDERSTOOD – THE CHALLENGE OF EMOTIONAL SUFFERING

CHAPTERS 4-7: LET THE VERBAL SPARRING BEGIN!

"In God I trust and am not afraid. What can man do to me?" - King David in Psalm 56:11

Nicknamed the "Machine-Gun Preacher," the author received his blue belt in kickboxing!

<u>**Summary And Insight**</u>: Experience does not equal "doctrine."

In Job 4-7, the verbal sparring begins, as Job's three friends take issue with Job's angst-filled statements from Job 3. Instead of being compassionate, Eliphaz is upset at Job's intense emotions. In his opinion, Job has counseled others, so he should be able to handle his own emotions in a better fashion. (Job 4:1-6) Eliphaz argues that the wicked are destroyed, not the innocent and upright (4:7-11), even though every human being experiences trouble. In his opinion, Job should appeal to God to heal and rescue him by bringing his cause before him. (Job 5:8-26) From Eliphaz's perspective, these generalizations are fixed, universal truths which can be applied to Job's case. (Job 5:27) Eliphaz has neatly packaged God as one who must act according to his understanding. After all, if the innocent never perish, and if God hears their appeals, all Job has to do is pray and be healed! Eliphaz never stops to think how presumptuous it is to limit God by his own feeble reasoning. How foolish are the many "Elphazes" among us, whose assurance is, "If you only have enough faith you will be healed." If misapplied, these generalizations are simply superficial, harmful, wrong and very hurtful!

Eliphaz's argument is also flawed in that the Scriptures prove that the innocent do perish! Saul's godly son, Jonathan, died with his wicked father. (2 Samuel 1:4) Bathsheba's righteous and noble husband, Uriah, met an unjust end through the manipulation of King David. (2 Samuel 11:17) The lesson from both accounts is that we must be careful not to utter pious platitudes which "seem" to preserve God's honor, but we do so at the expense of the truth.

Eliphaz claims his views are supported by: (1 Experience (Job 4:8), and (2 Dream-like, ghostly revelations. (Job 4:12-16) Each is a questionable source of truth. Just because our experience may have resulted in a certain outcome, it does not mean that it becomes "doctrine" for everyone else. Eliphaz's notion to **"appeal to God"** is presumptuous, as he assumes that Job has not sought God. The advice to "just pray about it" must seem very trite to someone who has been pouring out his heart to God in utter anguish.

From Job's perspective, he is in anguish, frustrated and hopeless, because it seems that his friends have not really heard him, and God has assaulted him. (Job 6:1-13) He has asked his friends for nothing but their devotion – yet has gotten advice that challenges his integrity. (Job 6:14-30) In the face of a fate that is truly worse than death, Job will not

70

retreat to platitudes, but insists on facing ultimate questions honestly. (Job 7:1-11) Verse 11 is a key verse as it challenges every disciple to ask honest questions and not just put up a bold front. (Proverbs 21:29)

Looking now toward Heaven, Job cries out to God, *"... Why have you made me your target? Why do you not pardon my offenses and forgive my sins?"* (Job 7:20b-21a)

What do we take away from these chapters? Hurting people need compassion and gentle discipling, not pontificating speeches. The challenge for them is to appreciate the "targeting" of God – although it brings pain – it will ultimately draw them closer to him. (Romans 8:28)

Lessons In Being Discipled: Faith And Trust

While the Book of Job is considered by many to be an "exposé of suffering," it is also a remarkable case study in "discipling" – God's plan to train and transform his people through the Biblical counseling of other godly men and women. (Matthew 28:18-20) As we explore chapters 4-37 in the Book of Job, we are going to examine the painful emotional lessons that are taught, both in taking discipling from and giving discipling to other human beings. It is here that three cycles of "speeches" begin between Job and his three friends, and we are reminded of the invaluable Scripture in Proverbs 18:2, *"Fools find no pleasure in understanding, but delight in airing their own opinions."* One of the key mistakes of counseling that we will see in this "discipling case study" is that Job's friends refuse to acknowledge Job's integrity and seek rather to accuse him of hypocrisy. After attempting to be patient, Job finally gives into his weakened state and responds in anger and sarcasm. Proverbs 22:24-25 states, *"Do not make friends with hot-tempered person, do not associate with*

71

one easily angered, or you may learn their ways and get yourself ensnared."

While every disciple of Jesus must "seek to understand" and be slow to anger in dealing with challenges in relationships, we cannot be so sensitive that we are unable to appreciate the "spiritual sparring" that may occur. Proverbs 27:6 states, *"Wounds from a friend can be trusted but an enemy multiples kisses."* Will we ever be wounded by bad or hard advice given by a well-meaning heart? Sure. The goal is to trust the heart and appreciate the "silver-lining" in spite of the flaws. Sometimes, unless things are put in such a gentle way as to train a four-year old child, some adults feel offended. (Proverbs 19:11) This is due to a lack of mental toughness and recognition of "tough love." People who do nothing but appease are not helpful, but harmful. We must have the courage to say what needs be said, even it may be hard to hear. I have heard it said that the difference between a "harsh talk" and a "hard talk" is the addition of faith. The same issues need to be brought up, but the person who is harsh may lack the faith to believe that the person can change. As the Scriptures communicate in Romans 14:23b, *"Everything that does not come from faith is sin."*

At the same time, we must have the balance to not be naïve or lack a spiritual "filter." I have also heard it said, "If you accept everything, you are no better than the city sewer!" As a result, we must also be discerning in gaining wisdom. Proverbs 14:15 reveals, *"The simple believe anything, but the prudent give thought to their steps."* The challenge is to trust that God is always working through his Spirit in disciples of Jesus, yet the mouthpiece through which his word comes may be flawed. Essentially, we need to be able to "eat the fish and spit out the bone!" In other words, we are to trust the word of God completely, and value the experiences

72

and skills of our disciplers, not as doctrine, but as sound advice that if collaborated by the word of God is beneficial.

As a member of our former fellowship, the International Churches of Christ, I experienced a sincere effort to call all disciples to obedience to the Scriptures. However, some began to enforce discipling in a top-down style that made the "disciplee" feel guilty if they did not immediately obey any advice given, even if it was against their conscience. Even sincere and respectful questioning at times was considered "prideful." Sadly, this ignores a foundational element in discipling relationships, shared by Jesus:

> *Jesus called them together and said, "You know that the rulers of the Gentiles Lord it over them, and their high officials exercise authority over them. Not so with you. Instead, whoever wants to become great among you must be your servant, and whoever wants to be first must be a slave – just as the Son of Man did not come to be served, but to serve, and to give his life as a ransom for many."* (Matthew 20:25-28)

The relationship between a discipler and "disciplee" is one of respect and mentorship as we see in the relationship between Apostle Paul and his son in the faith Timothy. (Philippians 2:19-22) While there is an authority component with disciplers due to the need to satisfy the needs of the church, the relationship must exude love, patience and respect. (1 Thessalonians 5:12-13) When disciplers stop seeking to understand and only seeks to lord over disciples with their opinions, they lack love and become like *"a resounding gong or a clanging cymbal."* (1 Corinthians 13:1) Over the years, the discipling relationship matures into a more of an adult/adult relationship and less teacher/student, although there is always a leader of the two for the sake of unity and direction. The example of this is seen in Paul's relationship with Silas, an older Christian who was sent out with him to deliver the message from the Council at Jerusalem for the Gentile disciples to obey. (Acts 15:22) The growth in the discipling paradigm is important for the recognition of spirituality over the years, and is one in which I enjoy with Kip McKean as I continue to learn from him through my leadership of the AFRICANUS (Africa and the Mid-Atlantic USA) World Sector. Sadly, one of the downfalls of our former movement was the lack of growth and respect in discipling relationships, which often led to bitterness and resentment.

In Job 4-7, we see that Job has the spiritual maturity – in spite of unbelievable physical and emotional pain – to listen and respond to the advice of his three friends despite its flaws. This was another spiritual test – the test of religious persecution caused by the faulty doctrine of his three friends. Despite his spiritual maturity, Job made the mistake of allowing his frustration with the assumptions of Eliphaz's argument to cause him to give into anger and unwholesome speech. This reminds me of Proverbs 26:4-5, which states, *"Do not answer a fool according to his folly, or you yourself will be just like him. Answer a fool according to his folly, or he will be wise in his own eyes."*

Are these two Scriptures contradicting the other? Absolutely not. The difference is in the reaction. If we respond to sin with sin, then we have already given into temptation and the Devil's trap. Galatians 6:1 admonishes, *"Brothers and sisters, if someone is caught in a sin, you who live by the Spirit should restore that person gently. But watch yourselves, or you also may be tempted."*

What is the temptation? Frustration and anger. Like Job's wife's admonition to *"curse God and die,"* we can also want to *"curse"* discipling if we have been hurt in the past by bad advice or harsh correction. Sadly, it was the abandonment of discipling in the former International Churches of Christ that caused multitudes of disciples to leave the Lord. Discipling became an ugly word. It became at best, "optional" and in most cases, non-existent. The Devil's plan to use such "unjust suffering" to justify an abandonment of a Biblical premise was "masterful." Despite our circumstances, however, we must keep our eyes on the cross. As 1 Peter 2:18-19 stresses, *"Slaves, in reverent fear of God submit yourselves to your masters, not only to those who are good and considerate, but also to those who are harsh. For it commendable if someone bears up under the pain of unjust suffering because they are conscious of God."*

David, before God made him Israel's King, displayed this heart to love despite the challenge in his relationship with King Saul. When tempted to harm King Saul, David became conscience-stricken. In 1 Samuel 24, David was on the run from Saul. Then, David found himself to have the element of surprise as Saul happened to relieve himself in a cave where David and his men were hiding. Here is this amazing account:

> *[David's] men said, "This is the day the Lord spoke of when he said to you, 'I will give your enemy into your hands for you to deal with as you wish.'" Then David crept up unnoticed and cut off a corner of Saul's robe. Afterward, David was conscience-stricken for having cut off a corner of his robe. He said to his men, "The Lord forbid that I should do such a thing to my master, the Lord's anointed, or lay my hand on him; for he is the anointed of the Lord." With these words David sharply rebuked his men and did not allow them to attack Saul. And Saul left the cave and went his way.* (1 Samuel 24:4-7)

Wow! What incredible integrity toward an enemy who would have surely killed David had Saul had the chance! David's heart is truly the heart of discipling. While our disciplers may not be "kings," they have been chosen by the leadership to meet the needs of flock, as Jethro advised Moses. (Exodus 18:13-26) While they may not have the authority of the Lord, they have been given the responsibility to serve his people. The qualifications of such people are also important, as it is the leadership's responsibility to *"select capable men (and women) from all the people – men (and women) who fear God, trustworthy men (and women) who hate dishonest gain."* (Exodus 18:21) Does this describe the character of the disciples who have been entrusted to disciple the souls of your church? Does every person who has the privilege of discipling others understand just how significant of an impact it can have? We must not give the Enemy an opening and lead our young members astray due to our negligence.

A Lesson From Kickboxing: "Know Pain, Know Gain."

Using sports terminology, discipling is the "coaching" that is necessary to groom and train any "spiritual athlete."   In February of 2015, I came to a crossroads in my spiritual fitness and decided to get some urgent "discipling/coaching." Despite playing various sports, running and going to the gym on a regular basis, I still weighed 235 pounds on my 6 foot frame. I could have justified my state due to stress resulting from a hectic schedule, but I decided to "honor God with my body." (1 Corinthians 6:20) Instead of becoming content in being a little "plump," I made the decision to go back to my marital arts roots and find something in my neighborhood where I could be trained and "pushed" beyond my perceived limits. I needed some hard and even "unjust suffering" to burn the weight off! After some research, I found a 7:00AM Dutch Kickboxing Class that met three times a week. It was part of a mixed-martial arts gym that was owned by Antoni Hardonik, a former UFC fighter, who had trained great current fighters such as Ronda Rousey, the first USA woman

76

to earn an Olympic medal in judo at the 2008 Summer Olympics in Bejing and a former UFC Women's Bantamweight Champion. Under the tough conditioning and talented focus of my kickboxing coach, AJ Barnala, I lost over 50 pounds in a year and 6 inches on my waist! It was remarkable! I had always considered myself to be a serious athlete, but it was not until I was trained beyond my perceived limits that I achieved the success I desired.

The writer of Hebrews states, *"See to it, brothers and sisters, that none of you has a sinful, unbelieving heart that turns away from the living God. But encourage one another daily, as long as it is called, 'Today,' so that none of you may be hardened by sin's deceitfulness."* (Hebrews 3:12-13) In order to achieve the weight loss I desired, I needed to believe that I could lose the weight. I needed to believe even in the midst of training that the sprints and leg matrix exercises that I dreaded would be for my benefit. This was the "silver lining" – the vision through the storm that I needed to focus on. I needed to believe that the sparring sessions where I could literally take a "controlled beating" would replace my fear with courage. I needed to believe and trust that AJ had my best interests at heart instead of being a sadistic foreman barking orders not to stop! I decided to believe and get the help. So every Monday, Wednesday and Friday from 7:00AM – 8:15AM, we would persevere through a 15-20 minute warm-up that felt more like a boot-camp; a training session where we would practice drills until the sweat was literally making puddles at our feet; a sparring session to face different types of opponents for several rounds; and finally – if you were up to it, and most of us were – another 15 minutes of sprints, leg matrix or clinch drills, sparring to the point where almost everyone collapsed on the floor out of sheer exhaustion. We had become warriors – in AJ's words, "Beasts!" By the time of my blue belt exam, I was at the point where I could spar experienced amateur fighters with several fights under their belt – and survive! In AJ's inspirational adage, "Our cool-down is the world's workout!"

The same relates to our spiritual walk with God. Do you trust your Coach? Do you trust that God has your best interests at heart even when you feel like you are going through the most perilous of times? Do you trust that God will put people in your life who are trustworthy and capable to help you reach your goals?

In his letter to the church in Rome, Paul writes through the inspiration of the Spirit, *"I myself am convinced, my brothers and sisters, that you yourselves are full of goodness, filled with knowledge and competent to instruct one another."* (Romans 15:14) Later to the church in Colossae, he writes, *"We proclaim him, admonishing and teaching everyone with all wisdom, so we may present everyone perfect in Christ."* (Colossians 1:28)

These Scriptures remind us that every Christian – regardless of their maturity – should be eager to allow trustworthy disciples to help "coach" them in their "fight" to defeat Satan and become more like Jesus. This practice of humility is vital since a person's *"heart is deceitful above all things and beyond cure. Who can understand it?"* (Jeremiah 17:9) Before I had lost the weight, I had deceived myself into thinking that my eating habits could be overlooked. That needed to change. I had deceived myself that I could handle my own fitness and I did not need coaching. That needed to change. Where are you today? If we are not getting better, we are getting worse. There is no such thing as a "spiritual plateau." Since we are incapable of effectively counseling ourselves, the need for competent disciples to help us keep Jesus at the center of our attitudes and our actions is necessary to be *"made holy, useful to the Master and prepared to any good work."* (2 Timothy 2:21) Are humans perfect? Of course not. But we have a perfect plan with the word of God. The goal is for every Christian to become a coach, a discipling partner, by learning how to teach. As Paul states to his son in the faith Timothy, *"And the things you have heard me say in the presence of many witnesses entrust to reliable people who will be qualified to teach others."* (2 Timothy 2:2)

To trust God and those in our lives is not an easy matter, especially when the trials of life are burdensome or unfair. In the Book of Job, we see the Ultimate Coach offer Job as an example of integrity to battle Satan's schemes. In Job 1:7-8 the Scriptures educate, *"The Lord said to Satan, 'Where have you come from?' Satan answered the Lord, 'from roaming throughout the earth, going back and forth on it.' Then the Lord said to Satan, 'Have you considered my servant Job?'"*

What? Why would the Lord "volunteer" Job to be tested by the most powerful demonic archangel in the universe? To prove Satan wrong? To glorify his name? To help Job grow through trials? This is unjust suffering at its clearest! Job had no idea that what he was about to go through had been allowed by God and implemented by Satan. Relating this to a kickboxing and boxing analogy: It is one thing to train with a more experienced fighter who had your best interests at heart and wanted to make you better. It is another experience entirely to be put into a ring with a "spiritual Mike Tyson" of sorts – the Devil, who like Mike Tyson, literally wanted to knock your head off your body! Yet Job would trust in the sovereignty of God – his ultimate Referee and Coach – despite being misunderstood and falsely accused by his "loyal" friends.

Throughout the Bible, we see its heroes endure unjust suffering through a gamut of reactions that led to significant breakthroughs in their understanding of the sovereignty of

God. In the Book of Psalms, we find kings and servants who react to suffering with anger in their hearts, revenge on their minds, or even despair in their emotions, all the while knowing that God is in control of their destiny. Job, in reaction to his own suffering, demonstrates that there simply is no easy relationship between good fortune and righteousness, or between misfortune and wrath. Jesus himself describes the sovereignty of the Father in Matthew 5:34b, *"He causes his sun to rise on the evil and the good, and sends rain on the righteous and the unrighteous."* Job finds that life is a mystery that can be faced only by trust and reliance upon God. This mystery eludes the easy answers of his companions and even his own best explanations. It defies Job's reason and shatters the boundaries of his understanding – as it does our own. Let's jump into the practicals and learn how to be more faithful for the Lord!

CHAPTERS 8-10: DESPITE UNFAIR CIRCUMSTANCES, GOD IS STILL JUST

This classic – *Job Rebuked By His Friends* – was painted by William Blake in 1805.

The humble sinner will sometimes be interpreted as one of the filthiest in the eyes of man yet immersed in the eyes of God, and this is due to the volition of honesty regarding his own corruption. - Criss Jami[14]

Summary And Insight: Tradition does not equal truth.

Bildad now joins in this condemnation of Job with blunt accusations. (Job 8:1-22) In his perspective, since God does not *"pervert justice,"* the death of Job's children is proof that they sinned. (Job 8:2, 4) This view of God is extremely

---

[14] Jami, Criss (2015). *Killosophy.* CreateSpace Independent Publishing. p. 70.

legalistic. There is no room in Bildad's theology for God's mercy or grace. To Bildad, our walk with God is a business transaction. If your balance sheet shows sin, God will come after you like a creditor in search for his money! The lesson here is that in discipling, we must avoid making rigid simplistic statements about God. Bildad's comments about relying on "the former generations" show that he puts his trust in tradition as the authority for his views. If a teaching was accepted by the ancients, it must be correct. In discipling, our standard must be Scripture itself, not what others have said about it.

The issue of the death of Job's children's as proof of Job's sin and their own must have been very hurtful to Job. This situation was also seen in my former fellowship of the ICOC, especially when the child of leaders "fell away." My dear friend, Kip McKean, drew the brunt of this criticism, yet through faith was able to overcome this severe trial. Ron Harding – the historian of the SoldOut Discipling Movement – records this in his book, The Chronicles Of Modern-Day Christianity (p.53):

> At the beginning of 2001 as a college student in Boston, the oldest of the McKeans' children began to question her faith. Though everyone who falls away must take full responsibility for this decision, it must be noted that this young woman was unjustly and heavily criticized – largely because of the high profile of her parents. This feeling of being unloved by key leaders in the congregation contributed to her no longer attending church in April 2001. (Luke 17:1-2) This single event caused uncertainty in the McKeans' leadership among many of the World Sector Leaders, as well as among the Kingdom Elders and Kingdom Teachers. So, in September of 2001, the World Sector Leaders "compelled" the

McKeans to go on sabbatical – though later, some deeply regretted this decision.

...Cited incorrectly to Kip and Elena was Proverbs 22:6, "Train a child in the way he should go, and... he will not turn from it." Disregarding what is obviously implied in the phrase, "when he is old," is that during their younger years children may not be faithful to God, but will return to the Kingdom because of their good training when they are "old." (This has now been seen in the SoldOut Movement and the ICOC over and over again.) Even sadder is the lack of grace by almost all of the World Sector Leaders, Kingdom Elders and Kingdom Teachers. In the Scriptures, some of God's and Israel's greatest leaders had unfaithful children – Aaron, Samuel, and even the Old Testament's "man after God's own heart," David – yet they continued to victoriously lead "all Israel."

As Ron Harding in his eye-witness account reveals, it was the ungodly misinterpretation of the Scripture Proverbs 22:6 and a focus on the Mainline Church of Christ tradition that an unfaithful child disqualifies a father for leadership that caused the travesty of Kip being unjustly "removed" from leading the then Movement of God. This is the same lack of grace and mercy that we sadly see with Bildad. (I might add, as God vindicated Job, so likewise he vindicated Kip. The ICOC fell away from so many doctrinal truths of God's word such as discipling is a command of Jesus. Consequently, the ICOC ceased being a dynamically growing movement, but became merely a lukewarm and dying fellowship. Yet God raised up Kip – humbled by his suffering and God's great mercy – to lead God's "New Movement!")

Bildad continues that God comes to the aid of the *"pure and upright"* and *"does not reject a blameless man."* (Job 8:6, 20) We can almost sense Bildad struggling not to blurt out

83

what his argument obviously implies – Job has sinned, or he would not be suffering as he is. Job agrees with Bildad's premises – God does not pervert justice, and he does not reject the blameless. However, he takes the position, *"But how can a mortal be righteous before God?"* (Job 9:2) In his view, God, the vast, the distant, the unknowable is in fact tormenting him, and Job has no recourse. (Job 9:3-11) Job, having abandoned all hope, has nothing to lose since God cannot be called into court and questioned. (Job 9:12-20) Whether Job proclaims his innocence (and thus challenges God's justice) or puts on a pious face and pretends, he is doomed. (Job 9:21-35) Job's words obviously express despair, but also suggest a fascinating insight that even Job does not seem to recognize. When life seems unfair, the issue is seldom one of guilt or innocence. All pain is not punishment. And all the innocent are not blessed with health and wealth.

Job takes this opportunity to be honest and cry out before God. (Job 9:1) Again, he turns to God, and asks, "Why? With what sin am I charged? Do you enjoy oppressing me? Why is the Creator destroying His own creation?" At this point "guilt" and "innocence" seem meaningless terms for Job as he is being crushed. (Job 10:2-17) In Job's heart, it would have been better if he had never been born! (Job 10:18-22) I can only imagine that listening to all of this must have been uncomfortable for his three friends. When it comes to discipling others, most of us hurry away, afraid that the darkness of depression and despair will swirl around us as well. As a result, many hurting people, dreading that reaction, put on a smiling mask on their faces to hide the pain. Job's character of integrity does not permit this. He knows his friends will not *"hold me innocent,"* therefore he decides to be totally honest in expressing his thoughts and emotions. (Job 10:28) In the process, Job will force his friends to face the realities they fear – but which will ultimately lead all three friends and Job himself to a truer knowledge of God.

What do we take from all of this? We can know God is just and still admit that life is often unfair. The God-given freewill of every human being is not controlled by him, or else our wills would cease to be free! The challenge to reconcile this fact while dealing with the unfairness of life does not justify religious pretense that does not honor God. Do not change your expression and smile in your distress in order to placate others. Be honest and open about how you feel so you can get the help you need.

CHAPTERS 11-14: BEING CONFIDENT WITHOUT BEING DEFIANT

Job And His Friends by Gustave Doré

Summary And Insight: Assumptions are foolish and costly.

Zophar, Job's third friend, now contributes a lecture (Job 11:1-12) and a sermon. (11:13-20) He lectures Job for claiming to be right and pure in God's sight (11:1-4), and if God spoke up, God could produce evidence to show Job has not even received what his sins deserve! (Job 11:5-6) Zophar believed that if God punishes, the sufferer must be guilty. (Job 11:7-12) Once again we see a clear condemnation of Job from his "friend." Zophar has become Job's judge and jury. In a discipling relationship, this is a key issue. As Paul admonishes us in Romans 14:13, *"Therefore, let us stop passing judgment on one another."* While we are called to *"judge those inside the church,"* we must not allow our judgments to be made out of a faithless or critical heart. (1 Corinthians 5:12) To quote my friend Tim Kernan, "A good leader must have a critical eye, but not a critical heart."

Then comes Zophar's sermon, a classic example of proclaiming irrelevant truth. The paraphrase: *"Be devoted to the Lord. Pray. Stop sinning. Then everything will be fine."* (Job 11:13-16) What a dagger in the heart of a man who has been devoted to God, but is suffering anyway! And what pain Zophar's description of divine blessing must have caused. (Job 11:17-20). This is exactly what Job's life was like – and all has been lost, in spite of the fact that Job is not at fault.

Job's response is complicated. Job asks why is he suffering rather than the wicked? (Job 12:1-6) This is really Job's problem. He already knows the truisms that his friends have expressed – and discovers that they do not apply in his case! He has been forced to realize that the ways of God are mysterious. God is free to act and does act, not limited by finite human understanding. What bothers Job is that God seems to act in ways contrary to what he and his friends have always assumed about him. Surely all nature lies in the hand of God!

As a result, Job is confident in stating that God is too vast for any man to comprehend, and that he acts with sovereignty and does what he pleases. (Job 12:7-25) Job challenges his friends on their use of maxims to unjustly smear his character and their attempt to take the place of God in their judgment of him. (Job 13:1-12) Job's desire to speak to God shows that he is not willing to abandon his faith. Instead he wants God to explain his suffering. This example of calling out "why" is far better than saying, "Because I do not understand, I will not believe." This is the answer to the old argument which states that if God is both good and all powerful then when something bad or unfair happens, we must either doubt the goodness of God or his sovereignty.

Job's friends have no evidence that he has committed any unrepentant sin, yet they call him a sinner. The Law of Old Testament was clear that a thorough investigation of eyewitness testimony is necessary to be accepted in court.

> *If a malicious witness takes the stand to accuse someone of a crime, the two people involved in the dispute must stand in the presence of the Lord before the priests and the judges who are in office at the time. The judges must make a thorough investigation, and if the witness proves to be a liar, giving false testimony against a fellow Israelite, then do to the false witness as that witness intended to do to the other party. You must purge the evil from among you.* (Deuteronomy 19:16-19)

Therefore, it is clear that Job's friends "speak wickedly" on God's behalf due to their presumption. (Job 13:7) If only Job could face God in court, he would be vindicated. (Job 13:13-19) Job asks only for two things: 1) That God will stop tormenting him, and 2) Job will have a chance to defend himself. (Job 13:20-28) Instead, Job is helpless before God. (Job 14:1-6) From his perspective, death is his only hope. His only comfort is the assurance that in time God will remember him and he will be raised, his sins forgiven. (Job 14:7-17) However until then his hope is gone. (Job 14:18-22)

Even though Job discusses the resurrection, his speech ends in sorrow. In that world, he still has no hope and no future. What do we get from this? A confident surrender and trust of God's sovereignty and mercy is necessary, not worldly sorrow. When we are hurt, it is important to remember that God is not our adversary; he is still on our side.

CHAPTERS 15-17: HOLDING ON TO INTEGRITY FOR ANOTHER "ROUND"

**Boxers Bernard Hopkins and Joe Calzaghe
"clinching" during a round!**

Summary And Insight: Do not expect God to explain; just hold on to your integrity.

Eliphaz begins a second round of dialogue. Angry and upset, he accuses Job of undermining piety with irreverent talk. (Job 15:1-6) This is a common issue in discipling relationships, as some disciplers are shocked that anyone would ask questions about matters of faith. To express doubt or uncertainties, or to struggle with difficult questions, is viewed as an attack on God. As I was sharing my convictions with a Nigerian lawyer who was helping us setup our church incorporation in Lagos, she stated that asking questions about religion in Nigeria is considered heretical. She said, "Only blind acceptance is required." When I shared about the nature of true discipleship with her, she was encouraged. We must remember that God is great enough to "survive" our questions and doubts. Anyone who is honest in his or her struggle to understand God is far more likely to come to faith than lose it. The person who truly undermines piety is the one who insists that others should be satisfied with superficial or pat answers, is unwilling to face difficulties, and is afraid to ask questions.

Unfortunately, Eliphaz launches into a series of questions designed to shame Job and accuse him of arrogance. (Job 15:7-13) Eliphaz's own "religious vision" has convinced him that man is vile and corrupt. (Job 15:14-19) He then launches a poetic description of the fate of the wicked, who futilely attack God (Job 15:20-26) or ignore him in favor of wealth and pleasure. (Job 15:27-35) His speech contains several cutting remarks, referencing what has actually happened to Job. (Job 15:21, 28, 29, 30, 34) Eliphaz's hostility reflects his view of an untrusting God who mechanically and impersonally lays out punishments that are not tempered by compassion or love. There is a cruel dogmatism in his speech that does not accurately reflect the heart of God.

Indignantly, Job strikes back. He rebukes his friends for being *"miserable comforters."* (Job 16:1-5). The Hebrew definition of a "miserable comforter" is literally a "comforter of trouble," a person who makes matters worse rather than better.[15] Such phrases as, "What could you have done to deserve this?" and "If you had enough faith, you would be healed," are typically examples of modern miserable comforters. The modern sufferer, like Job, needs reassurance

---

15

https://www.blueletterbible.org/lang/lexicon/lexicon.cfm?Strongs=H5999&t=NIV

that God loves him or her and that even though many times we cannot understand the "why" of suffering, we care.

Job now asserts that he has not attacked God, but God has attacked him. (Job 16:6-14) Job has not been corrupt but pure. (Job 16:15-21) He pleads with tears for an advocate and an intercessor, which could also be interpreted as a Messianic prophecy for Jesus, given its resemblance to Isaiah 53:11-12. Job has experienced the tragedies that struck him as a violent attack. And his "attacker" has been God! Yet, as Job describes his reaction, we realize that he has not denied God, nor struck back at him as Eliphaz implied. (Job 15:23-26) Rather than shake his fist at God, Job humbled himself, wept and prayed. No wonder God described Job as a *"blameless and upright"* man. (Job 1:8; 2:3) Despite Job's confusion, he has continued to act righteously. When we can do what is right despite pain, pressure and agonizing loss, we are truly godly individuals.

However, Job's spirit is broken by his suffering and the conviction that God, the only One who can vindicate him, will not do so during his lifetime. His only hope lies in the grave. (Job 17:1-6) Job uses the language of ancient business contracts and asks for some "pledge" (down payment) from God as security for his vindication that will definitely come. (Job 17:3) Only God can demonstrate Job's innocence and despite his despair and ambivalence he believes in God's justice.

Aside from his anguish, Job continues to hold on to his faith. This act of "holding on" is an important aspect for all of us as Christians. It is through endurance that our faith is proven genuine. Jesus speaks to this issue in John 8:31-32, *"To the Jews who had believed him, Jesus said, 'If you hold to my teaching, you are really my disciples. Then you will know the truth, and the truth will set you free.'"* In this passage, the faith of the Jews was not enough. Their emotions would waver unless they decided to build deep convictions by holding to the standard of God. How about you? Are you holding on to God in faith or wrestling him in fear?

The example of Jacob's wrestling with God is a prime example of the value of the struggle in the midst of loneliness. In Genesis 32, Jacob is left all alone after his family and possessions are sent over across the Jabbok River.

> *So Jacob was left alone, and a man [the Angel of God] wrestled with him till daybreak. When the man saw that he could not overpower him, he touched the socket of Jacob's hip so that his hip was wrenched as he wrestled with the man. Then the man said, "Let me go, for it is daybreak." But Jacob replied, "I will not let you go unless you bless me." The man asked him, "What is your name?" "Jacob," he answered. Then the man said, "Your name will no longer be Jacob, but Israel, because you have struggled with God and with humans and have overcome."*
> (Genesis 32:24-28)

The struggle is necessary for the blessing. Unlike the "stop and go" impact of boxing, the constant "holding on" of wrestling can wear you down to the point where you have nothing left. It is at that moment where your integrity is revealed. You can either let go or hold on. That is the difference between "losers" and "overcomers." The latter have the endurance for the struggle. The former do not.

TESTIMONIAL: OLOLADE ORIOWO

My name is Ololade Oriowo, and I am a former student of the University of Lagos. In fact, I was baptized on April 1, 2018 in Lagos! After I became a disciple, I received "a lot of flack" from my siblings. Taiye and Kehinde – my brother and sister – were not interested in studying the Bible at all. Kehinde, my younger sister, was simply interested in doing her own thing and living her own life. While Taiye, her twin brother, though he liked the fact that I knew the Bible, was taken aback at my being radical and "changing churches." He said I lacked wisdom, telling me that I need "to play both sides" – my parents and the church – so there can be peace in the house. Likewise, he accused me of being disrespectful to my parents by being a member of a church that was not my parents' church thereby "dividing" our family.

I vividly remember one such time on the 31st of December 2018. There is a tradition in Nigeria's false doctrine churches called "Watch Night" or "Crossover Night" where everyone flocks to church on the night of New Year's Eve to pray in the New Year. Since I refused to go with my family to attend this event, Taiye came into my room raining insults on me, calling me names, and accusing me of dividing the family. He then started dragging me and pushing me to the car by brute force. My sister, in addition to insults, declared that she would never go with me to church and would never become a disciple. Most of the persecution that I suffered was slander and name-calling by my siblings, while my parents "tagged" me as a "bad child." I never disrespected my parents but because I took a stand against attending a church that does not preach true Biblical doctrines, it was perceived as disrespectful.

Despite the ill-treatment from my family, I continued to reach out to and encourage my siblings to study the Bible. I asked Taiye to study the Bible, but he refused because he was discouraged by the "stress" (persecution) I was enduring from the family, which included himself. I asked a brother in the Lagos Church to reach out to him, since Richard was a family friend with whom Taiye was quite comfortable. It took a year for Taiye to eventually start studying the Bible, as he remained afraid of persecution and our parents. Then like many, he almost quit studying the Bible as he saw the commitment that a disciple must have to follow Jesus. He eventually stuck with the studies and worked through his fears, and on March 21, 2019, he was baptized into Christ!

Kehinde decided to visit the church after Tolani and Kate (the Lagos Campus Ministry Leaders) visited my home during a campus break, as Kate had a great conversation with her. Taiye's interest in the Bible had piqued her curiosity, and by the grace of God, on May 12, 2019, Kehinde was baptized as a disciple of Jesus Christ! I am so glad that my siblings became disciples despite all the persecution that I faced through them. After seeing our godly examples, our parents became very supportive of us! I am so proud of my siblings – who are shining examples for the Lagos Church – as they travel over two hours on public transportation to be at all the meetings of the body!

In 2019, I received an academic scholarship to study Chemical Engineering at the prestigious Howard University. I am thankful to be part of a movement of churches as I am now part of the dynamic Washington DC Campus Ministry! Excitingly, Taiye and Kehinde have also been accepted into Howard for the Fall Semester of 2020! They plan to study Computer Science and Nursing respectively! Please pray for all three of us to excel both spiritually and academically, so that our parents will be inspired to be baptized making my whole family united in Christ! Lastly, I am so grateful for Dr. Drew, Patrique and the Lagos disciples who set the foundation for my life in Christ. Thank you for this opportunity to share!

Taiyo (left) rejoiced after being baptized by Richard!

Lolade (left) baptized her sister Kehinde! (center)

Lolade, Kehinde and Taiyo – physical and
spiritual siblings!

The author is so proud of his granddaughter
in the faith – Ololade!

CHAPTERS 18-19: OUR REDEEMER LIVES AND WE WILL SEE HIM!

Pray for God to give you the patience of Job!

Summary And Insight: Fix your hope on eternity and nothing can overcome you.

In Job 18:1-4, Bildad – as insensitive as ever to Job's feelings – is angry that Job considers the three friends' advice "stupid." Sadly this is a key issue in discipling. Too many people claim to be sensitive, yet they are only sensitive to their own feelings, not to the feelings of others. It does not matter that others may be hurt. If they feel insulted, they strike out viciously, trying to hurt. They see things only in black and white: Either completely right or completely wrong. They have forgotten Solomon's admonition in Proverbs 19:11, *"A person's wisdom yields patience; it is to one's glory to overlook an offense."* Instead, Bildad launches into a tirade in which he pictures the terrifying fate of the wicked, trying to "bludgeon" Job into surrendering to Bildad's traditionalism. (Job 18:5-21) Bildad's criticism focuses on the externals – on what happens to a wicked person. His sermon does reflect the tragedies that have struck Job but misses the mark by assuming that the loss of his material possessions and family tragedies indicate personal unrighteousness. Bildad needs to learn a lesson Jesus phrased succinctly, *"Life does not consist in an abundance of possessions."* (Luke 12:15) What happens within us is more important than any material consideration.

Job cries out in the pain of his humiliation. (Job 19:1-5) Job's inner strength remains unmoved, yet his anguish is rooted in his conviction that God has wronged him. (Job 19:6-12) The injustice of it torments him, an injustice that has *"stripped me of my honor."* (Job 19:9) Even *"little boys scorn me; when I appear, they ridicule me."* (19:18) Job's closest friends detest him and refuse him any pity, and his loved ones have turned against him.

The next verses are stunning in their affirmation of Job's unshakable faith. Rather than change a word he has uttered, he wants each one to be recorded forever. (Job 19:23-24) This is because the very God who allows Job to be tormented is his Redeemer! Job finds joy in the truth that on one future day, Job will see the Lord with his own eyes and so will be vindicated. (Job 19:25-27) It is interesting to note in verse 25 that Job speaks of "my Redeemer," who was known to him as his goel, or "vindicator."[16] This Hebrew word designated a close relative who is responsible for making sure that justice has been given to his kinsman. The position of the pronoun in the sentence is emphatic: *"I know that my Redeemer lives."* Despite all that has happened to Job and despite his conviction that God has treated him unfairly, Job still believes

---

16

https://www.blueletterbible.org/lang/lexicon/lexicon.cfm?Strongs=H1350&t=NIV

that God will redeem him! Whatever doubts Job has, and whatever thoughts he had expressed to his three friends, Job is a man of resolute faith. This is a reality of which Job's friends lack understanding, but we must imitate this "resolute faith" during our times of doubt.

Although Job doubts that he will be vindicated in this life, he has no doubt that he will be resurrected and stand before God. He yearns for that time, when *"I myself will see him with my own eyes."* (Job 19:27a) Then the torment and suffering will end. What a bright promise the resurrection has for us all! As the Scriptures states about Jesus in Revelation 21:4, *"He will wipe every tear from their eyes. There will be no more death or mourning or crying or pain, for the old order of things has passed away."*

As for his friends, they should have been much more careful in what they said to Job. Falsely accusing Job will not go unpunished! (19:28-29) It is this "hounding" and judgment that is wearing down Job's spiritual muscles as he continues to hold on to his integrity. Paul reminds us of the dangers of this action:

> *You, then, why do you judge your brother or sister? Or why do you treat them with contempt? For we will all stand before God's judgment seat… So then, each of us will give an account of ourselves to God. Therefore, let us stop passing judgment on one another. Instead make up your mind not to put any stumbling block or obstacle in the way of a brother or sister.* (Romans 14:10-13)

Let us be honest: We have known "disciples" who like to pass judgment. (We usually cannot see this character sin in ourselves.) They are self-righteous, pontificating individuals who are eager to express their viewpoints to anyone who will listen. Sadly, this is a common occurrence among the religious. Jesus points to this in his parable of the Pharisee and the Tax Collector in Luke 18. The lesson in discipling is clear: We must have a humble attitude in dealing with others, so that we do not become a stumbling block to their repentance and growth. As Jesus states in Luke 18:14b, *"For everyone who exalts himself will be humbled, and he who humbles himself will be exalted."* It is easy to be contemptuous when we are thinking that we are better than others. At all times, there is opportunity for us to think of others better than ourselves. (Philippians 2:3)

The challenge for Job in all of this is to remain patient and hold on to his hope in God. If we fix our hope in eternity, nothing that happens in our brief lifetime can overcome us. God and his standard will not be mocked... even if we are.

CHAPTERS 20-21: REALITY OFTEN CHANGES POPULAR BELIEFS

**A Middle Ages depiction of *Job And His Friends*
by Kievan Psalter. (1397)**

Summary And Insight: God always has an answer –
sometimes one we do not expect!

Zophar is disturbed by Job's view and only in part because it
"dishonors" him. (Job 20:1-3) Job's view is disturbing to
Zophar because it attacks his shared conviction with Bildad
that God always punishes the wicked. This conviction is not
only basic to Zophar's view of a moral universe, but in
Zophar's mind, it is critical to maintain an ordered society.
Underlying Zophar's beliefs is the fact that he is well off.
When wealth comes, it is natural to assume that we are

affluent because we are good. If we are secure, we are tempted to believe that it is because we deserve to be. The poor and oppressed, however, work under no such delusion. The wicked often take advantage of the righteous poor, and the exploited of this world know the wicked may prosper and the good suffer. Any honest view of reality must take this into account, no matter how "disturbing" it may be.

Zophar reaffirms the doctrine that "the joy of the godless last but for the moment," and that in the end *"distress will overtake"* the wicked. (Job 20:5, 22) Job's response must have been even more alarming. Job confesses his terror at the thoughts his personal tragedy has awakened. (Job 21:1-6) All of Job's life, he has shared the views expressed by his three friends. The disasters that stripped him of everything have forced Job to rethink not just some, but all of his beliefs. Indeed, it is frightening to challenge beliefs on which we have based our whole lives. Yet some experiences force us to do so. Job contradicts Zophar by arguing that in fact many wicked do live an almost idyllic life. (Job 21:7-16) Job sketches an almost idyllic portrait of the life of the wicked. They live to old age and prosper, yet they consciously reject God. Given that their *"prosperity is not in their own hands,"* Job cannot understand the rationale behind this. (Job 21:16) Job quotes his friends' acknowledgement of this by saying, *"God stores up punishment of the wicked to their children."* (Job 21:19) All man really knows is that death is the great equalizer.

> *One person dies in full vigor, completely secure and at ease, well-nourished in body, bones rich in marrow. Another dies in bitterness of soul, never having enjoyed anything good. Side by side they lie in the dust, and worms cover them both.* (Job 21:23-26)

Job's friends have accused him of not listening. Yet in Job 21, he quotes or alludes to several of their arguments and refutes them. For example, in Job 21:9, Job refutes Bildad's words in Job 18:19 saying the wicked's *"homes are safe and free from fear."* Some people assume that if we do not agree with their opinions, we have not listened. Job restates the arguments of his friends to show he was listening and then goes on to disagree. This is a key issue in discipling that can cause much misunderstanding and bitterness. People tend to agree for the sake of peace even though there is no true unity.

Job's friends have taken his calamities as proof of some hidden wickedness. Job's reply concludes the second cycle of dialogue and shows their position is nonsense. (Job 21:27-34) If the wicked may prosper then there is no "quid pro quo" relationship between suffering and punishment. Therefore what happened to Job is not proof that he is wicked, and so the argument of Job's three friends collapses. The problems, however, remain. Why has God subjected Job to suffering? Why does God not immediately punish sin?

In Psalm 73, God gives us an insight not available to Job. There the Lord shows us that the apparent prosperity of the wicked is fleeting.

This is what the wicked are like – always free of care, they go on amassing wealth. Surely in vain I have kept my heart pure and have washed my hands in innocence. All day long I have been afflicted, and every morning brings new punishments. If I had spoken out like that, I would have betrayed your children. When I tried to understand all this, it troubled me deeply till I entered the sanctuary of God; then I understood their final destiny. Surely you place them on slippery ground; you cast them down to ruin. How suddenly are they destroyed, completely

105

swept away by terrors! They are like a dream when one awakes; when you arise, Lord, you will despise them as fantasies. (Psalm 73:12-20)

Job faces these facts, despite the challenge they pose to his understanding. What's the lesson here? Be ready to face disturbing facts that you may not be able at the moment to understand, but never abandon your faith... in other words, be like Job!

CHAPTERS 22-24: GOD'S JUDGMENTS CAN BE MYSTERIOUS AND DELAYED

We must keep our hope in the sovereignty of God!

Summary And Insight: Trust God's timing and God's way.

Eliphaz intensifies the pressure on Job, whose arguments seem incomprehensible. How can any man's meaningless life benefit God? (Job 22:1-3) The question implies that God is not personally involved with individuals – that he stands back, impartial and gives out punishment and reward simply because it is his role as the moral judge of humanity. The perspective of Eliphaz moves from general statements about the wicked being punished to accusing Job of being a swindler, a robber and lacking hospitality! (Job 22:4-9) He then concludes with an impassioned plea to repent. Apparently then the impartial, almost mechanical God that Eliphaz believes in will deliver. (Job 22:21-30).

In the Old Testament world, truth was established by witnesses and punishment followed. Here Eliphaz is reasoning backward. Job is being punished, therefore God must have "witnessed" Job's sinful acts. Carrying Eliphaz's reverse reasoning to a logical conclusion, the sins that God witnessed of Job must be heinous, such as oppressing the weak, murder, adultry or being contemptuous towards God.

There is only one problem with Elpihaz's logic: He was completely wrong! Eliphaz's God is impersonal, uninvolved and self-contained. His God does not value man or take personal pleasure in man's actions. This is not true of our God. In Job 1 and 2, God expresses his pleasure in Job, as *"blameless and upright, a man who fears God and shuns evil."* (Job 1:8) Through Job's integrity, Satan was defeated and Job glorified the Lord. The truth is clear: When we live for him, the Lord is both pleased and glorified. What is the lesson in discipling? Never accuse or condemn your brothers and sisters based on circumstantial evidence. You will probably be wrong as many times as you are right, and in the process hurt others just like Eliphaz.

Job moans in deepening despair, yet he seems to be making spiritual progress. Earlier, he seems to have demanded a trial to showcase this injustice. Now Job simply yearns to *"find out what [God] would answer [him], and consider what he would say to [him]."* (Job 23: 5) In Job's heart of humility, he does not believe God is unjust, even when he seems to be acting unjustly. In this, as in earlier affirmations of his character, Job is an example to us. We may well be asking "why" as Job does. We may also be facing the apparent inconsistencies between human experience and the nature of God; yet, we must also be humble enough to believe God does have an answer, even though we may not know what it is. It takes spiritual maturity to affirm, "I do not understand why I am in this situation, but I trust God absolutely."

What may also tempt Job to be contemptuous is that God is acting in a way in which Job, as well as Eliphaz, confidently believed he should not. (Job 23:13-17) In fact, Job's suffering

108

has forced him to pose a theological problem that he and his friends have not only ignored, but denied could even exist. Why is there poverty and oppression? Why are the wicked permitted to prey on the powerless? (Job 24:1-17) Although the wicked eventually die, why does God permit them any *"rest in a feeling of security,"* since *"his eyes are on their ways?"* (Job 24:23)

The key to this section is Job 24:1 – *"times for judgment."* Job does not question God's justice, only his timing. Very often this is an issue for many disciples. They do not agree with the timing of God. One of my favorite Scriptures in regards to this is Solomon's admonition:

> *Since a king's word is supreme, who can say to him, "What are you doing?" Whoever obeys his command will come to no harm, and the wise heart will know the proper time and procedure. For there is a proper time and procedure for every matter, though a person may be weighed down by misery.* (Ecclesiastes 8:4-6)

Although God's timing may cause us misery whether we understand or not, we must trust in the providence of God. If we are wise and trust in the Lord with all of our heart and not our own understanding, we will be able to discern the proper time and procedure for what must be done.

Unfortunately, Eliphaz's traditionalism assumes a "knee-jerk reaction" from God; Eliphaz assumes that God reacts immediately to sin. Nevertheless, the New Testament reminds us, *"The Lord is not slow in keeping his promise, as some understand slowness. Instead he is patient with you, not wanting anyone to perish, but everyone to come to repentance."* (2 Peter 3:9) Also consider, *"The sins of some men are obvious reaching the place of judgement ahead of them; the sins of others trail behind them."* (1 Timothy 5:24) What is the challenge for us? Remain firm in your conviction that God will right every wrong, but in his own time and in his own way.

INTERLUDE: THE JOSEPH PRINCIPLE: FLOURISHING IN TIMES OF FAMINE

As we study the Book of Job, one of the most important character traits of Job that is revealed is patience in the face of trials. In my opinion, the example of Joseph in the Book of Genesis is one of the most inspiring examples of patience through suffering that I have seen in the Bible or in life. Since God wanted to teach Jacob, his father, to be surrendered to his will, I believe that God decided to extend that lesson to his son Joseph, as well as to build Joseph's faith!

If you study out the beginning of Joseph's life in Genesis 37, you will see that his walk with God started with dreams – dreams that neither he nor his family could understand. His brothers became jealous of him because his dreams made it seem like they would be subject to him. In time, they concocted a scheme that ultimately sold him into slavery. At this point Joseph was only 17 years old! He was a teen! Can you imagine how Joseph must have felt? It would have been easy to feel that his family had turned their backs on him and God had abandoned him. But that was not the heart of Joseph. By Genesis 39, we see several points that can be gleaned from his character.

Summary And Insight: Be excellent no matter the reward.

Did Joseph get depressed by being sold into slavery? Did he lose faith in God and stop obeying him? Absolutely not! Joseph held onto God, not because of any evidence that it would prove beneficial, but because of his personal faith and integrity. Other people would have been angry and questioning God, but Joseph focused on doing his best for God. This pursuit of excellence was rewarded as Joseph was promoted in his master's house. However, because of

Potiphar's unrighteous wife, Joseph was falsely accused of attempted rape and lost everything. His decision to refuse her sexual advances is one of the most shining examples of integrity in the Bible.

At this point, Joseph had gone for literally years without the influence of family or spiritual fellowship. Imagine no discipling, no spiritual mentoring, no fellowship for years... How would you respond? It would have seemed to most people that God had abandoned Joseph. As a young man, his hormones would have been at their peak. The possibility of fulfilling his sexual desires would have probably been tempting him in the extreme! However, what was his heart in this? Genesis 39:9 states, *"How then could I do such a wicked thing and sin against God?"* He had received no spiritual encouragement or direction besides the convictions he gained as a boy growing up in a Hebrew home. Now, far away from that home and its influences, he maintained his purity for God, even though no human was looking over his shoulder to check up on him. He was all alone. So how does this relate to us?

Examine yourself spiritually and ask yourself the following questions: How long does it take for me to lose faith and give up on God? Without the Bible, without fellowship, without physical or spiritual family, what would I have done? How well am I doing now with the benefit of all those things? Am I grateful for the Kingdom? Am I getting the most out of it to help myself and others? If I was all alone, with no one to help me, how sold-out for God would I be?

In Philippians 2:12-13, the Bible states, *"Therefore my dear friends, as you have always obeyed – not only in my presence, but now much more in my absence – continue to work out your salvation with fear and trembling, for it is God who works in you to will and to act in order to fulfill his good purpose."* We need to work out our salvation with fear and trembling, both in the presence of the church and when we are alone! Who we are when we are all alone is who we really are! We must all trust that God is always working according to his good purpose in our lives.

After being thrown in jail for refusing to violate the law of God, Joseph had a choice to make. He could either become faithless and bitter or spend himself in the pursuit of excellence. What is amazing to me is that he again "stayed the course" with God in spite of having absolutely no spiritual influence outside his own faith. No church service, no Bible, no righteous fellowship – nothing! As he had been promoted to run his master's house, he ended up overseeing the affairs of the jail in which he was a prisoner. Cream always rises to the top! But another major disappointment was on the way! By Genesis 40, there were more lessons to be learned.

Summary And Insight: Be faithful no matter the obstacle.

Joseph's faith was not based on what others could do for him! His faith was completely in God! While in prison in Genesis 40, Joseph interpreted the dreams of two officials – the chief cupbearer and the chief baker – both of whom had offended the Pharaoh. Joseph's interpretation of their dreams proved to be true, as the cupbearer was restored to his position and the chief baker was executed. Unfortunately, the cupbearer became sidetracked by the joy of his release and did not remember Joseph's request to speak to Pharaoh on Joseph's behalf. Surely Joseph would now begin to question the God who was allowing all of these injustices! If he did at all, it was not for long. Indeed, Joseph's faith and good deed was forgotten by a man, but Joseph knew he was not forgotten by God. He was sold-out for God with a faith based not on reward, but on surrender alone.

Sometimes, we question whether God is looking out for us when things do not go the way we would like, or we question when other people do things that may hurt us. Romans 8:28 is emphatic, *"And we know that in all things God works for the good of those who love him, who have been called according to his purpose."* Do your convictions weaken because of the actions of others? Even disciples? We need to be surrendered to the fact that God never stops working for those who are committed to him!

Being uptight and lacking trust is a poor choice when God has promised to work out all things for our good. The cost of discipleship is unconditional surrender, but the dividends are joy and peace. If things do not happen the way you plan or would like, do you get stressed and anxious? God allows our plans to change to test our reliance on him, and not on ourselves. Over the past 12 years, the Spirit has "blown" my family from Syracuse, New York to Washington DC to plant a new congregation for our Movement; then from Washington DC to Los Angeles, California to train with Kip and Elena and to build the LA Campus Ministry; then from Los Angeles, California to New York City, New York to rebuild a hurting and weak church; then back to Los Angeles to strengthen contemptuous situations that had threatened two regions of the church; then the big move to Lagos, Nigeria to experience third world church building; and then and only then, to plant Johannesburg, South Africa – the pillar church for the entire African continent! It is remarkable to note that during all of that time, our goal had been to plant the church in Johannesburg. However, the Spirit delayed that plan, and thus, we were forced to trust God's will and God's timing. The first Scripture that I ever memorized still speaks volumes in my life today, Proverbs 16:9, *"In their hearts, humans plan their course, but the Lord establishes their steps."*

God's plan for his church is obvious. He will continue to prune the tree so that it can be *"even more fruitful."* (John

15:1)   He has cut off those who were unwilling to be surrendered to God's plan and instead chose to settle and build their own tower to glorify themselves. Remember: God blesses according to his timing! Is your faith based on God or his miracles? Do you see God's wish to prosper us before it comes? As for me, I am focused on doing the work of God. Satan may want you to get dejected over the lack of repentance of people you are reaching out to, but instead, focus on your own repentance and fruit will come! There are others in the world who are spiritually dying and need help! What are you doing for God? So inspirational is Habakkuk 3:17-18, *"Though the fig tree does not bud and there are no grapes on the vines, though the olive crop fails and the fields produce no food, though there are no sheep in the pen and no cattle in the stalls, yet I will rejoice in the Lord, I will be joyful in God my Savior."*

<u>Summary And Insight</u>: Be patient no matter the wait.

How patient are you willing to be before you lose faith and give up on the waiting for God to move? Remember his promises, and do not let your temptations of sensuality stop you from remembering the truth. Stay joyful and know that it is God who gives us the strength to continue! Can your patience with God stand the test? Psalm 27:13-14 states, *"I remain confident of this: I will see the goodness of the Lord in the land of the living. Wait for the Lord; be strong and take heart and wait for the Lord."*

Joseph was sold into slavery at age 17. Jailed falsely while being absolutely pure. Forgotten by a man who owed him his life. Approaching age 30 after 13 years of frustration and disappointment, he could have blamed it all on God and retreated into himself. Yet he held on to God. He became better, not bitter; more faithful, not faithless; dedicated, not doubtful; righteous, not resentful. What was the result? Besides the 13 years of ill treatment? By chapter 41, Joseph became second-in-command of the greatest nation the world had known at that point in history – Egypt! In the process, he saved his own family through which God was going to bless the world. During all of the difficult years, he was not campaigning for the "vice-presidency of Egypt." He was not even aware the office was "up for grabs." He only knew that God was God, whether times were grand or grueling, and he held on for dear life.

Often our patience with God is put to the test with the passage of 13 days, and severely tested in 13 months. The thought of patiently waiting on God to act for 13 years is in a word – overwhelming! We have so much to learn from Joseph. He truly lived by faith, and not by sight because his eyes were on God and not on his circumstances. (2 Corinthians 5:7) He remembered the promises of God! (Psalm 105:17-23) Joseph's heart was a heart that was grateful to God, looked to him for strength, and remembered the wonders he had done!

How do you serve God? What benefits do you hope to receive? How much of your dreams are tied to personal recognition and accomplishment? The moral of Joseph's life is doing right with or without rewards. This is how you flourish in the face of famine. Do your best, and trust God will take care of the rest. Serve because you love him, and give him free rein to do with you what he thinks is best. Joseph did not serve to gain recognition; he served only to please his God. In order to trust God and be patient, we need to remember that God's patience means salvation. (2 Peter 3:15) If God was not patient, we would not be given an opportunity to repent of our sins. As a result of his grace and mercy, he wants *"all people to be saved and come to the knowledge of the truth."* (1 Timothy 2:4) So decide to imitate Joseph's faith. No matter the obstacles help this very lost world to see the life of Jesus – a life of excellence, a life

116

of faith, and a life of patience, because Jesus believed in the power of God.

A quote that has steadied my walk in midst of trials is from Dr. Martin Luther King Jr. In 1963 during the intense days of the American Civil Rights Movement, he declared, "The ultimate measure of a man is not where he stands in moments of comfort and convenience, but where he stands at times of challenge and controversy." Pray that when God measures our lives, we will not be found wanting.

CHAPTERS 25-28: BACK TO BASICS, BACK TO FAITH

The daunting painting of *Job And His Three Friends*
by James Tissot. (1899)

Summary And Insight: Trust God's wisdom.

In Job 25:1-6, Bildad's brief speech concludes the discourses of Job's friends. Bildad holds that God establishes order in the material and moral universe. As he shines brighter than anything in creation, man in comparison is an immoral worm. Therefore, all of Job's claims of purity are meaningless.

Job dismisses Bildad with scathing sarcasm. (Job 26:1-4) In powerful poetry, Job affirms God's majesty. We can hardly comprehend even the *"outer fringe"* of God's greatness, much less squeeze him into the friends' comfortable categories. (Job 26:5-14) Man is no maggot to God. For some, it's a theological teeter-totter: If God is to be exalted, man must be degraded. Job saw this as terribly wrong. As disciples, only in Christ do we truly realize how wrong Bildad actually was! Christ chose to become a real human being, *"made lower than the angels,"* but raised again to bring *"many sons and daughters to glory."* (Hebrews 2:9-10) God's love for us proves that we are not maggots. God's love marks us out as beings of infinite worth!

Despite the false accusations of his friends, Job maintains the justice of his cause and keeps on affirming his integrity. (Job 27:1-6) I can only imagine the temptations Job faced to say what they wanted to hear. Likewise in discipling, we can be tempted to do the same, rather than to fight to keep a clear conscience. A pious attitude often covers up an aching heart or painful doubts. Job had taken a courageous course and refused to desert it. We now see that, however great the pressure, Job strived to be totally honest with God and totally honest with others. The fierce honesty that Job chose did not produce any easy or quick answers. Yet in the end, it won commendation from God. Job's friends, who had spoken so "learnedly" of divine judgment, are now themselves in danger. (Job 27:7-12) Job concludes as his friends have begun... God does, most certainly, punish the wicked. (Job 27:13-23)

In Job 28, Job's interlude describes human advances in technology though they lack the wisdom to fear God. (Job 28:1-28) Even in Job's time, mankind had demonstrated amazing technological proficiency. Metals were mined and smelted, tunnels drilled through the rock, and the sources of rivers and streams explored. The mysteries of the material universe have fallen one by one to the probing genius of humanity. Today an explosion of technological advances makes us wonder if there is anything in this universe humanity cannot master. The problem is that technological advances are not matched by advances in wisdom – here defined as the capacity to penetrate the moral mysteries of the universe. In the moral realm, man is utterly lost and totally inadequate.

Job and his friends struggled to apply their concept of God and his justice to Job's experience with suffering – and ultimately failed completely. And so the author asks, **"Where then does wisdom come from? Where does understanding dwell?"** (Job 28:20) The answer is that God understands, and **"He alone knows where it dwells."** (Job 28:23) All a man can do is to fear God and to shun evil. (Job 28:28) God is the source of wisdom in the moral universe even as he is the Creator of the material. What we cannot grasp, God knows completely. Far too many people are quick to make moral pronouncements: Homosexuals march for pride; Abortion is merely a matter of a woman's personal freedoms; Sex educators distribute condoms to teens, but never mention abstinence. They all loudly proclaim that their position is "moral" while ignoring God's understanding as expressed in Scripture. The only hope is to abandon human notions of morality and be subject to God. The wisest man that ever lived put it this way, **"Now all has been heard... Fear God and keep his commandments, for this is the whole duty of man. For God will bring every deed into judgement, including every hidden thing, whether it is good or evil."** (Ecclesiastes 12:13-14)

CHAPTERS 29-31: TURMOIL EVEN IN SURRENDER

Summary And Insight: It is better to suffer for good than for evil.

Job's dialogue with his three friends is complete. Now a lengthy monologue begins a swift movement towards the book's conclusion, much like a lawyer's final summation of a case. Job first describes his former life. (Job 29:1-25) He was rich and respected (29:1-17), confident and secure. (29:18-25) Now he is mocked and detested by others (Job 30:1-14) and emotionally shattered. (30:15-31) He cries out to God, but receives no answer, and as the days of suffering lengthen, *"the churning inside me never stops."* (30:27) Job affirms that he has always acted righteously, with the unmistakable conclusion, at least in his mind, that what is happening to him is unfair.

Chapter 29 has a distinct and interstesting pattern: Blessing (29: 2-6); Honor (29:7-11); Job's compassion (29:12-17); Blessing (29:18-20); Honor (29:21-25). Job merited the blessings of his earlier life and the respect of his friends, because he showed compassion for the needy and lived a just life. To demonstrate the unfairness of God, Job takes each of the themes he introduced in chapter 29 and contrasts his past and present state in chapter 30. Now Job is mocked by young and old (Job 30:1-8) and verbally attacked. (Job 30:9-15) Now there is no blessing from God, but only suffering (Job 30:16-17) and affliction (Job 30:18-19), no matter how urgently Job pleaded. (Job 30:20-23) Perhaps worst of all, there is no compassion for one who constantly showed compassion for others. (Job 30:24-31) In Job's mind, no matter how great his suffering, there is never mercy.

The Book of Job exhibits a strong sense of social as well as personal morality. In Job 31:13-21, these verses display several characteristics of morality displayed in social justice:

Treating employees fairly (v. 13)

Meeting the needs of the poor (v. 16)

Strengthening the widow (v. 16)

Sharing with the fatherless (v. 17)

Seeing that the needy are clothed (v. 19)

Obtaining justice for the poor (v. 21)

The Bible clearly teaches that those who have the resources are responsible for meeting the needs of the helpless and protecting others from legal oppression. There is a Biblical "social gospel" of good news – those who love God are to demonstrate it by showing active compassion for the needy. I am very proud of the Lagos Church, as we were able to start a MERCY*worldwide* Signature Project with The Real School (primary level) in Okobaba, Nigeria! Okobaba borders Makoko – the largest "marine slum" in the world.

Okobaba painted by the Nigerian
artist – Mufutau Apooyin!

Job's final words reveal a self-righteousness attitude as he fights to be surrendered to his fate. (Job 31:1-40) Job describes the sins he believes to be worthy of punishment with "if then" statements, essentially continuing to argue why his suffering in unfair. According to Job, if he had turned aside from God's pathway (as he defined it), he would deserve his present suffering. He further defends his integrity that if God were to weigh him with *"honest scales"* – implying that the evaluation of his character is flawed – then God would know he was *"blameless."* (Job 31:6) After stating his case, Job falls silent. His surrender is not based on an acceptance of God's sovereignty, but a lack of his own understanding.

CHAPTERS 32-37: SUFFERING CAN HAVE A REDEMPTIVE PURPOSE

Elihu Addressing Job - Anonmous

Summary And Insight: Accept the mystery of God's ways and remain unshaken in trust.

With the Middle East's characteristic respect for age, Elihu has remained silent while his elders have debated. Now they have fallen silent, and Elihu is eager to have his say. (Job 32:1-22) In his lengthy discourse, Elihu often quotes Job's words and questions specific views Job has expressed. (Job 32:11-12; 33:1, 31; 34:5-7, 35-36, 35:16) His humility is clear, as he states, **"I am just like you."** (Job 33:6) It must have been refreshing for Job to hear from someone who does not think of himself as morally superior. Anyone engaged in discipling must come with Elihu's attitude. We are all clay. We struggle together. Only a humble person, who rejects the temptation to condemn or hold others in contempt, can be God's agent to heal and bind up the wounded.

Notice that Elihu is not arrogant in challenging Job, as Job's three friends were. He does, however, make clear that Job is *"not right."* (Job 33:12) Elihu quotes Job's words, not to condemn him, but simply to point out an error in his thinking. (Job 33:9-11) There is no attack here, no assumption that Job must have sinned terribly to be suffering now. It is not a sin to be wrong, even when we are wrong about an important issue. Job has claimed that he did not consciously sin, and Elihu will not refute that. Yet because one did not sin consciously or willfully does not mean he or she is sinless! (1 Corinthians 4:4)

One of the issues that underlie the arguments of Job and his friends is the logical reasoning that if A = B and if B is true, then A must also be true. Job's friends believe A (that God punishes sin) with B (suffering and loss). Elihu's contribution is to point out that C may also be equal to B. That C (God instructs human beings) through B (suffering and loss). Since A = B and C = B, neither Job nor his friends can hold that B always means A, since B perhaps means C. God's purposes are so complex; perhaps B is also equal to D, E, F, G and H!

Elihu's alternative to the logic which led the three friends to insist Job must have sinned – and led Job to the agonizing conclusion that somehow God must be acting unjustly – is crucial to breaking the circular reasoning of their arguments. Elihu looks outside their train of thought to recognize that God may use suffering redemptively. The point that *"God does speak"* in different ways is an important aspect of Elihu's comments to teach Job the power of God's sovereignty. (Job 33:14) God used "sovereign suffering" to "speak" to us even during this time of COVID-19, which has resulted in the drawing many pagans and Christians alike to a deeper reliance on God. He also communicates through his word, other disciples and prayers, as we seek his will through life's challenges.

Pain may awaken a man to spiritual danger and direct his thoughts to God. (Job 33:19-28) In this case, suffering is a blessing in disguise – much like the pain sensors of our skin inform us of cold and heat. Therefore, our conviction that God is good can survive despite the suffering of the innocent. This thinking is repeated in Elihu's reprise of Job's argument, but Elihu avoids the fallacy of applying this general principle to Job's case, while also reassuring him that he wants Job *"to be cleared."* (Job 33:32) He points out that God has at least one purpose in suffering other than punishment. The attacks of Job's friends fail, and Job need not torment himself with fears and thoughts that the God he trusts is unjust. In a grand conclusion, Elihu extols the wisdom and awesome majesty of God. (Job 37:1-24)

In essence, human beings cannot always reason from a past experience to pinpoint a purpose that God may have had in permitting it. Therefore the three friends, so secure in their condemnation of Job, were completely out of line. As well, Job was unnecessarily tormented by the doubt his own rigid theology caused. Though Job kept his integrity – as God promised – he did complain to God and his friends that God was unjust.

INTERLUDE: THE FURNACE OF AFFLICTION

Nelson Mandela is a revered hero to the author, to all of Africa, and to the entire world!

In 2009, the United Nations declared July 18th to be Nelson Mandela International Day. It was a privilege to experience it for the first time when our Johannesburg Mission Team arrived in South Africa on July 16, 2019. The day of July 18th is meant to encourage people everywhere to emulate Mandela's humanitarian legacy and recognize the decades he spent fighting apartheid. In South Africa, they honored Mandela's 67 years of public service with 67 minutes of charity and community action around the country.

Although Mandela spent 27 years of his life in prison for his speeches and activities against apartheid before being released in 1990, he was greeted as a hero upon his release for promoting a message of forgiveness and equality. Apartheid was abolished in 1991, and in 1993 Mandela was awarded the Nobel Peace Prize for his work. By 1994, South Africa held its first elections in which black people, as well as the white were allowed to vote. Mandela was elected as its first black President with the specific agenda to bring people of different races together. He even selected F.W. de Klerk, the former South African President, to be his deputy. One of my favorite quotes of Mandela that is so appropriate for our study of Job states, "Difficulties break some men but make others. No axe is sharp enough to cut the soul of a sinner who keeps on trying, one armed with the hope that he will rise even in the end."

Anne Bradstreet – a 17th century poet who was the first published author in America, female or otherwise, once wrote, "Iron till it be thoroughly heated is incapable to be wrought; so God sees good to cast some men into the furnace of affliction, and then beats them on his anvil into what frame he pleases." In our 21st century vernacular, a more modern version of her quote would probably sound something like be this, "Until iron is thoroughly heated, it is incapable of being changed; so God knows that it is best to allow men to be in the furnace of affliction, and then shapes them on his anvil into the form that pleases him."

In Isaiah 48:10-11, God says, ***"See I have refined you, though not as silver; I have tested you in the furnace of affliction. For my own sake, for my own sake, I do this. How can I let myself be defamed? I will not yield my glory to another."*** The word translated ***"affliction"*** here has been variously rendered as "poverty" and "misery."[17] God uses miserable experiences in our lives to refine us and to purify our hearts.

Perhaps you may be going through trials and difficulties in your life. These are the days when our enemy the Devil is

---

17

https://www.blueletterbible.org/lang/lexicon/lexicon.cfm?Strongs=H6040&t=NIV

endeavoring to wear out the saints of the Lord! The good news is that we should not despair, because our God is sovereign, and cannot be mocked. (Galatians 6:7) We must resist the temptation to be self-reliant and leave ourselves in his hands, remembering that God will use all these trials, oppressions and humiliating experiences to refine us, purify us and equip us to be effective and glorify him! The *"furnace of affliction"* is the proving ground of the Christian experience. Like my mother always used to say to me, "People are like tea bags. You don't know their flavor ...until they are put in hot water."

We often wonder why God allows us to go through challenges, even as strong Christians, yet even the world understands this wisdom. For instance, automobile companies – before sending out their new models – put them through rigorous tests. They have what they call their "proving ground," where their automobiles go through a punishing and grueling time of testing. This is necessary because they do not want the automobiles to break down after they are in use by the purchasing public with the potential to cause serious injury thus discrediting the company. So they seek to find out where the weaknesses are before they put them on the market. The same can be said for boot camp or training camp or any other preparation that serves to shape and strengthen the character and skill of the participant.

God deals with his people in much the same way. Testing times do come and will continue to come to the people of God. We will find ourselves in the furnace of affliction, oppression and humiliation so that our weak spots may be revealed and God can deal with them. The problem is that our pride stops us from seeing the weak spots. We do not like to acknowledge our failings. So God has to "hammer" us until we decide to humble ourselves underneath his hand

and accept his calling. He chooses us as we prove ourselves faithful to him in the hours of testing. The question for us is whether we are grateful and accept his refining process or whether we resist and reject it. Are you inspired to be in the furnace of affliction? Are we inspired to be "hammered" into the image of God?

In 1995, the author's mentor and friend Dr. Kip McKean (left) met with Nelson Mandela in Pretoria, South Africa!

I have heard it said that people are like the tools in a blacksmith's shop. They are either: 1) On the scrap pile, in desperate need of repair with no notion of purpose; 2) On the anvil, welcoming the painful pounding of the blacksmith's hammer, longing to be rebuilt and begging to be called; or 3) In their master's hands, responding to their Master's forearm, demanding nothing and surrendering everything. We are all somewhere in the blacksmith's shop, and some of us have experienced all three!

The analogy of the blacksmith's shop in relation to us is clear: The shop represents the world, we represent the item being made, and the blacksmith is clearly God, who wants us to be *"an instrument for noble (or better) purposes."* (2 Timothy 2:21) The reason why people are in the cobwebbed scrap pile, in desperate need of repair, is because they are clueless as to God's purpose for their lives. They are complacent, not asking the questions that are obvious, such as, "Why am I here?" "What happens when I die?" "Who is God?" "And what does God expect of me?" Instead they live self-satisfied lives, following the routine of life. Yet that is not what we are here to do! We are here to seek out how God wants to use us for his purposes. We are not here to be in the corner gathering dust. Now we are going to examine another place that we can be in the blacksmith's shop: On the anvil. The following is another excerpt from Max Lucado's *On The Anvil*:[18]

> With a strong forearm, the apron-clad blacksmith puts his tongs into the fire, grasps the heated metal, and places it on his anvil. His keen eye examines the glowing piece. He sees what the tool is now and envisions what he wants it to be – sharper, flatter, wider, longer. With a clear picture in his mind, he begins to pound. His left hand still clutching the hot mass with the tongs, the right hand slams the two-pound sledge upon the moldable metal. On the solid anvil, the smoldering iron is remolded. The smith knows the type of instrument he wants. He knows the size. He knows the shape. He knows the strength. Wang! Wang! The hammer slams. The shop rings with noise, the air fills with smoke and the softened metal responds. But the response doesn't come easily. It doesn't come without discomfort. To melt down the old and recast it as new is a disrupting process. Yet the metal remains on the anvil, allowing the toolmaker to remove the scars, repair the cracks,

---

[18] Lucado, Max (2001). *On the Anvil.* P. 47-48.

refill the voids and purge the impurities. And with time, a change occurs: what was dull becomes sharpened; what was crooked becomes straight; what was weak becomes strong; and what was useless becomes valuable.

Then the blacksmith stops. He ceases his pounding and sets down his hammer. With a strong left arm, he lifts the tongs until the freshly molded metal is at eye level. In the still silence he examines the smoking tool. The incandescent implant is rotated and examined for any mars or cracks. There are none. Now the smith enters the final stage of his task. He plunges the smoldering instrument into a nearby bucket of water. With a hiss and a rush of smoke, the metal immediately begins to harden. The heat surrenders to the onslaught of cool water and the pliable, soft material becomes an unbending, useful tool.

Do you trust the blacksmith's pounding as you lie on the "anvil of life?"

There Are Three Questions That Help Us Identify Our Spiritual Condition:

Are You "Bent Out Of Shape" Spiritually?

Have you ever felt like you are on God's anvil? I know I have. After coming out of the cobwebs of the world and offering myself to being used by God, his word pounded the sin right out of me. I needed Christians in my life to sharpen me by helping me to see the sin in my life more than ever before. (Proverbs 27:17) My pride and deceit had to be melted down, so I was placed on the anvil for reshaping! I had way too many rough edges. I needed the discipline of God. My sinful nature needed to be broken. In retrospect, I understand that

132

I had "bent myself out of shape." It was rough, and it can still be. Maybe you have been seeking God, but you have not allowed his word or godly people in your life to help shape you through him. God wants to shape you to be a disciple of Jesus before (AND after) you are plunged into the waters of baptism as a powerful instrument for God!

For those of you who are disciples of Christ, maybe you have hit a spiritual slump. Maybe your fire has gone out and you are drifting downward into the foggy valley of questioning and discouragement. Our motivation can wane. Our desire can become distant, and responsibilities can become burdensome. Passion and enthusiasm are long gone. That's anvil time! You have heard all the thoughtful words of help and encouragement but you are still hurting and wondering... You are about to be placed on the anvil. Are you allowing yourself to be molded?

Being on the anvil is being brought face to face with God out of the utter realization that we have nowhere else to go. It is not easy to be on the anvil. Anvil time is not to be avoided; it's to be embraced. It reminds us of who we are and who God is. We should not try to escape it. To escape it means that we are trying to escape God's way of shaping us into the instrument that he envisions us to be for him. We can even become bitter and resentful toward those who are trying to help us while on the anvil and fall away! (Hebrews 12:7-15)

In Matthew 21:42-44, Jesus preaches, *"Therefore I tell you that the kingdom of God will be taken away from you and given to a people who will produce its fruit. Anyone who falls on this stone will be broken to pieces; anyone on whom it falls will be crushed."* Either we get broken by our sin, or we get crushed by God! So if God has placed you on his anvil, be thankful. That means he has a great vision for your life and that you are worth reshaping to accomplish this vision.

How Do You Respond To Pain?

How do you respond to the pain in your life? Do you say, "Thank you sir, can I have another?" Or do you get angry and frustrated? As a martial artist, I am trained to defend myself, but Jesus did not retaliate to insults and persecutions. He entrusted himself to God. (1 Peter 2:23) How about you?

When a potter bakes a pot, he checks how solid it is by pulling it out of the oven and thumping it. If it "sings," it's ready. If it "thuds," it's placed back in the oven. The character of a person is also checked by thumping. Been thumped lately? Thumps are these irritating inconveniences that trigger the worst in us. They catch us off guard. They are not big enough to be crises, but if you get enough of them, watch out. (Late-night phone calls, flat tires, crazy deadlines, last-minute hospitality, etc.) Do you sing (literally) or do you thud? In Psalm 71:19-21, the Spirit proclaims, *"Your righteousness, God, reaches to the Heavens, you who have done great things. Who is like you, God? Though you have made me see troubles, many and bitter, you will restore my life again; from the depths of the Earth you will again bring me up. You will increase my honor and comfort me once more."*

There's nothing like a good thump to reveal the nature of a heart. The true character of a person is seen not in "the good times" and successes, but in the thump-packed drama of day-to-day living. Anyone can have a form of godliness for a moment, but the real test is the longevity of godliness. How long can you stay radical for God when times are hard? If you have the tendency to thud more than you sing, take heart: There is hope for us, "thudders!" Here are some practicals:

Begin by thanking God for thumps. James 1:2 states, *"Consider it pure joy, my brothers and sisters, whenever you face trials of many kinds..."* Chances are that God is doing the thumping. And he is doing it for your own good. So every thump is a reminder that God is molding you. (Hebrews 12:8)

Learn from each thump. Face up to the fact that you are not "thump-proof." You are going to be tested throughout your life. You are not perfect, you are going to blow it. That is okay. We just need to learn from our experiences or we will repeat them. Determine to learn from the thumps; you cannot avoid them. Look at each inconvenience as an opportunity to develop patience and persistence. Each thump will help you or hurt you, depending on how you use it. (Philippians 2:12-17)

Be aware of your "thump-slump." Know your pressure periods. For all of us there are times during the week that we can anticipate an unusual amount of "thumping." The best way to handle thump-slump times? Head on. Bolster yourself with extra prayer and do not give up. Remember, no thump is disastrous. All thumps work for good if we are loving and obeying God.

Did you ever play on the swing as a child? I had a blast... I used to stand on the swing seat and go for it! Children love to swing. There is nothing like it. I learned a lot about trust on a swing. As a child, I only trusted certain people to push my swing. If I was being pushed by people I trusted (like my dad or mom), they could do anything they wanted. They could twist me, turn me, stop me! I loved it! I loved it because I trusted the person pushing me. However, let a stranger push my swing (which often happened at school and picnics), and it was like hang on, baby! Who knew what this newcomer would do? When a stranger pushes your swing, you tense up, ball up, and hang on. It is no fun when your swing is in the hands of someone you do not know. Even though my back was to my dad, I trusted the fact that he would take care of me because I saw his shadow.

Who Is Pushing The "Swing?"

Psalm 91:14-16, the Bible states, *"Because he loves me, says the Lord, I will rescue him; I will protect him, for he acknowledges my name. He will call on me, and I will answer him; I will be with him in trouble, I will deliver him and honor him. With long life I will satisfy him and show him my salvation."* God wants to rescue you; to protect you; to deliver you; to satisfy you!

Do you trust the Lord? In the right hands, you can find peace... even in the storm. For those of us who have accepted the call to preach the word to a lost world, we too are bringing life to the desert of the world. The storms rage, and the temptation to quit and fall back into our sinful natures can be just a wave or two away! Others will respect our conviction, but do not have the faith to join us on the journey. Yet, we will have to dig down deep and stir the coals! We need to fan into flame the spark of faith that believes the world can be won in our generation. The testing of our faith develops the perseverance that matures and shapes us into the image of our God.

Where do you want to be? Do you want the cushy life of the world with no risks, no fears and a security in material things rather than in God? Or do you want to live a life on the edge – a life of training, of risks, of reliance on God when everything else fails – and a reward for eternity? That is the difference between living a lukewarm life or a faithful life. Let us step into the wind "head on" with our Master and not be distracted by the waves of doubt and fear. If you are bent out of shape spiritually, get a plan to get straightened out. If you

136

respond to pain with ingratitude decide to respond with thanks. If you fear what the future holds, remember "Who" holds the future in the palm of his hand. Enjoy the process of being on the anvil… You are being shaped to be used by God!

PART 3. THE COMPLEXITY OF HIS SOVEREIGNTY:

JOB'S DELIVERANCE DESPITE HIS BEWILDERMENT AT GOD – THE CHALLENGE OF SPIRITUAL SUFFERING

CHAPTERS 38-41: ACCEPTING THE REBUKE OF GOD

"Those whom I love I rebuke and discipline. So be earnest and repent." - Jesus in Revelation 3:19

Job Confessing His Presumption To God Who Answers From The Whirlwind was gloriously painted by **William Blake!**

<u>**Summary And Insight:**</u> When suffering comes, accept the discipline of God.

As we draw near to the conclusion of Job, now the unexpected occurs. God, of whom Job had complained was beyond reach, suddenly appears! Job soon discovers that God did not come to be questioned by Job. Instead, God poses two series of questions and challenges for Job to answer.

The first series disputes Job's knowledge of the physical universe, knowledge which God possesses. (Job 38:1 - 39:30) Job, greatly humbled, realizes how limited his knowledge really is. (Job 40:1-5) God asks Job, who cannot even master the physical universe, if he will question the Lord's command of the moral universe. (40:6-14) Mankind's limited authority over evil, as well as nature, must teach human beings not to claim greater competence than God in the moral realm. (40:15 - 41:34)

As we read God's words to Job, we recognize the irony of his questions as the tables are now turned: Job had asked questions that he had no right to ask. Now God was going to ask questions that he had every right to ask! In Luke 20, when Jesus was questioned by the self-righteous Pharisees, his response was so complete that *"no one dared to ask him any more questions."* (Luke 20:40) Job *"dared"* to question the sovereignty of God and received a strong but loving rebuke that reminded him that God's will was beyond his understanding.

> *Oh, the depth of the riches and the wisdom and knowledge of God! How unsearchable his judgments, and his paths beyond tracing out! "Who has known the mind of the Lord? Or who has been his counselor?" "Who has ever given to God, that God should repay them?" For from him and through him and for him are all things. To him be the glory forever! Amen.* (Romans 11:33-36)

The aformentioned Scripture reminds us that our attempt to search for understanding the will of God is beyond our "pay-grade." Ultimately, since our lives were given to us by him, we have no reason to be "repaid" by the knowledge of "why." It is God's prerogative. As Solomon states in Ecclesiastes 7:10, *"Do not say, 'Why were the old days better than these?' For it is not wise to ask such questions."* To his credit, Job understood this at the beginning of his trials. Job 1:21 shows that he understood this truth as he states, *"The Lord gave and the Lord has taken away; may the name of the Lord be praised."* However, over time, his need to search for the reasons behind his affliction led to an unrighteous attitude and bitterness of heart.

In his rebuke of Job, God does not explain why Job was suffering. After all, it is really not Job's place to demand that God report to him! The entire monologue by God has one purpose only – to challenge Job to have a humble and repentant heart. The Lord informs Job that he really does know what he is doing, even though Job may not. This, after all, is the essence of a relationship with God. The strength to face difficult times is not found in knowing why we must face them, but in the confidence that our great God loves us completely and that he is still "large and in charge."

Job was hurting because he was confused about who God was and questioned his personal relationship with him. It is not the solution to life's puzzles that evades us; it is the comfort found in the absolute assurance that God loves us and controls the circumstances of our lives. God accomplished the restoration of Job's confidence through his questions. In this way, the Lord brought peace to Job's troubled heart.

God's illustrations of the "behemoth" and the "leviathan" which are so vividly described here are perhaps the physical characteristics of the hippopotamus and the crocodile. (Job 40:15 - 41:34) Yet they seem to be used in a symbolic or mythical way, as monsters which represent the powers of evil existing in history and the present world.

Since God judges all wickedness (Job 40:8-14), even the behemoth is under God's control (Job 40:15-23), as is the leviathan. (Job 40:24-34) This symbolic interpretation is supported by other clearly symbolic uses of the leviathan to represent evil forces which God defeats. In Psalm 74:12-13, the leviathan is Egypt, defeated by God's intervention. In Isaiah 26:21 - 27:1, the leviathan, the spirit of evil, is unleashed at history's end. Man struggles futilely against evil. (Job 41:18, 25-29, 33) Only God can, and will defeat it!

TESTIMONIAL: BOLAJI AKINFENWA

"But I tell you that everyone will have to give account on the day of judgment for every empty word they have spoken." - Matthew 12:36

In this era of "fake news," it is important to separate gossip and deceit from the truth, even when it painfully applies to Christian leaders whom you would expect to apply the word of God to their lives. (Jeremiah 6:13-15) The following are my reasons for leaving my former fellowship (the International Churches of Christ – ICOC) after being baptized as a disciple of Jesus on 26th of January 1992 in Nigeria.

I was invited into the full-time ministry of the Lagos ICOC in 1998 to serve as a sector leader and later a regional leader of Surulere and also of Somolu/Mushin. While leading the Somolu/Mushin Region, I also oversaw the churches in the country of Chad, as well as the Benin ICOC (Edo State) in Nigeria.

While leading the Somolu/Mushin Region, there was a major crisis in the church in Ilorin (Kwara State), and my wife and I were called upon to move from Lagos to lead the Ilorin Church back to spiritual health. When we arrived, we realized that the former leader was using a "divide and rule" kind of leadership, to the point where the marrieds were divided from the singles, and the singles were actually planning to separate and start a new church! It took God's intervention in prayer, many lessons from his word, and much discipling to heal their hearts and help the church come back together as one! Yet God did it!

A Conspiracy In The Leadership

During our time in Ilorin, a leader from Lagos called me and said that he would love to come spend the holiday with us with his family. My wife and I were happy to welcome them, so we had a good time together. Later, I was baffled when he left for a leadership meeting in Lagos and seemingly told them that I was terribly "sick" and needed a "heart specialist!" In addition, he had stated that the Ilorin Church was in complete disarray – after the repentance of the church had been made abundantly clear.

As we continued to lead the Illorin Church and helped them to get their focus back on God, a disciple in the church told me that the former leader of the church had informed one of our family group leaders to go against my decisions and report back to him. Despite this divisiveness, I encouraged the brother that God was in control and not to give into worry, but to pray for his repentance. God's sovereignty was evident as the actions of the former leader were made clear and he was made to apologize for his sinful behavior. I forgave him and encouraged him not to allow Satan to fill his heart and sin against God and his great people.

Sadly, more lies continued regarding my leadership to the point where I felt compelled to resign. With a heavy heart I sent my resignation letter to the Lagos ICOC Lead Evangelist. Later, I was told that the leadership of the Lago ICOC was against him for accepting the letter without consulting them. For that reason he was sent to Illorin to tell me that the letter was not going to be accepted until I came back to Lagos for 6-8 months for "strengthening" before my decision to leave the ministry would be approved. However, when the Lagos evangelist arrived in Illorin, he never told me about the elders' concern or that I had this option. It was sad to see how the church that I had invested years of my life in the ministry – from 1998 to 2006 – had become a breeding ground of deceit and malice. Sadly, at this juncture, I realized that this church had stopped being the church I had been baptized into back in 1992.

The Destruction Of HOPE*worldwide* Nigeria

In addition to deceit and malice in the leadership, my decision to leave the ICOC was also based on the financial impropriety of their benevolent organization, HOPE*worldwide* Nigeria. In the beginning, HOPE*worldwide* was successful due to proper leadership and accountability in the 1990's. However after the Kriete Letter, the leadership lost their grip of HOPE*worldwide* and before long the percentage of the number of non-disciples working for the organization kept increasing. I felt terrible that the incredible opportunity that we had to reach out to the needy was lost, all because we had weak leadership who lacked the capability to properly guide the benevolence arm of the church. Eventually it was exposed that thousands of dollars in sponsorships by the Nigerian government had been squandered and mismanaged. Despite the complaints of many, the leadership refused to change and HOPE*worldwide* was officially disbanded in Nigeria, never again to be a non-governmental organization.

Is This The Kingdom Of God?

The church that I was baptized into in 1992 was a vibrant church, but after the Kriete Letter, doctrines were altered, convictions level dropped, discipling times were neglected, and reaching out to the lost was almost forgotten. People came to church to showcase their clothing attires and "mark register" (check in). Disciples stopped coming to Bible Talks because they "didn't feel like going," and people were getting married without completing marriage counseling! Some Christians even married non-Christians. As well, the heart to sacrifice in contribution greatly decreased and people stopped investing their talents into the kingdom.

At some point, I told my regional leader that we should count the cost with everybody in the region so that we would know who really wanted to be disciples and those who did not, but he said, "That can't be done." Later, I realized that a lot of the members did not know how to study the Bible with people – even the leaders! I suggested that we start an equipping class to train the members to have the courage to study the Bible with people, but that too was turned down. The spiritual pain made me feel like I could not continue in this environment. I wanted to be where Christ was the focus, not in a place where everybody was competing against each other from a worldly point of view.

The Leadership Was No Longer Spiritual.

When the Lead Evangelist moved to the Island Region of Lagos, I thought it was just like any other move, until we heard that the church bought an expensive furnished apartment for the Lead Evangelist. The church was not happy about this at all, and a lot of people voiced out their displeasure. The leadership of the church came up with the explanation that it was an "investment." This was obviously not the intention and exposed the worldliness in the leadership. There were many other options for the use of that money, as the Lagos ICOC had other regions where just a small portion of that money could have been used to buy land and build a modest place of worship in order to reduce their facility expenses. I pray those who have been led astray by materialism will "come to their senses."

I told my dear brother Dr. Drew that I was so grateful when the Lagos Mission Team from the International Christian Churches (ICC) arrived in 2016! I had been in the "wilderness" for years and had almost fallen away, and Andrew and his wife Patrique nursed my awesome wife Chinyere and me back to spiritual health. I also appreciate his consistent efforts to reach out to the Lagos ICOC despite their rejections at our invitations to meet the McKeans at our African Missions Conferences. Regardless, I thank God that I have found the kingdom of God again like in the days of old! What a privilege it is to be entrusted to lead the Lagos Church to *"even greater things"* in the future! I am grateful to have been rescued from my spiritual pain so I can help guide others to the truth. As Jeremiah 6:16a states:

> *This is what the Lord says: "Stand at the crossroads and look; ask for the ancient paths, ask where the good way is, and walk in it, and you will find rest for your souls."*

I am thankful to my God for the suffering of being in a spiritual wilderness because I now appreciate God's kingdom – in the SoldOut Movement – like never before!

The Smellies and Akinfenwas are dear friends and partners in the gospel!

147

CHAPTER 42: REPENTANCE BRINGS REFRESHMENT!

Job's fortunes were restored and his blessings
were doubled!

*"Repent, then, and turn to God, so that your sins may be
wiped out, that times of refreshing may come from the
Lord."* - Acts 3:19

<u>Summary And Insight:</u> The rewards of faith will surely
come.

Job responds to God's self-revelation and rebuke with utter
humility. Now that Job has seen God, rather than simply hear
about him, Job senses his own limitations, *"I despise*

myself." Job no longer questions or challenges God's justice *"and repent in dust and ashes."* (Job 42:1-6) Now that Job has seen God and surrendered to him, he no longer fears. He has no more questions. All his doubts have been relieved by the sudden vision of God in all of his greatness.

I believe Job repents because he finally understood how much he had drifted in his faith. As Hebrews 2:1 states, *"We must pay the most careful attention, therefore, to what we have heard, so that we do not drift away."* Although Job's trials may have been undeserved, it served to expose the cracks of his character of self-righteousness and independent thinking that could only be revealed through such challenges. Now Job had the opportunity to repent and help his friends to do the same! As Hebrews 10:23 states, *"Let us hold unswervingly to the hope we profess, for he who promised is faithful."* God was faithful to Job throughout his trials! The challenge for Job, and for us, is to *"hold unswervingly to the hope we profess"* in God's promises and sovereignty!

Next, God rebuked Eliphaz and his two companions. Unlike Job, they *"have not spoken the truth about me, as my servant Job has."* (Job 42:7) Mark this: Neither refusal to deal honestly with reality, nor dogmatic claims that equate one's own positions to God's, are honoring to the Lord. That said, God forgave the three – in response to the prayers of *"[His] servant Job."* (Job 42:9) Thus we see the impact of Job's repentance – his example served to help others. He could pray for his friends to repent of their self-righteous attitudes, because he himself has been reconciled with God and had repented of such thinking.

It is interesting to notice that Job's family also returned to him in mass to comfort him. Job 42:11 states, *"All his brothers and sisters and everyone who had known him before came and ate with him in his house. They comforted and consoled him over all the trouble the Lord had brought upon him, and each one gave him a piece of silver and a gold ring."*

Where were they all before? Why would they comfort and console him after the *"trouble that the Lord had brought on him?"* (Job 42:11) This reminds me of the mad dash for support from family members when someone hits the lottery, yet in this case, it was Job's relatives who gave him gifts! Why? Was it out of guilt and shame? Did they believe Job was in sin and therefore kept their distance out of respect for God's discipline? Whatever their reasoning, they all flocked to him, professing affection and interest, ignoring or probably excusing their long absence and neglect at the signs of his adversity. Sadly, it is true that being a family member does not necessarily mean friendship. The Scriptures state in Proverbs 17:17, *"A friend loves at all times, and a brother is born for a time of adversity."*

What happened to Job afterward? The author takes us years ahead, and reports that all the signs of divine blessing were restored. As the result of his overcoming such terrible trials, Job is blessed with double the amount of possessions and family than he had before! His repentance was rewarded! Job 42:11 declares, *"The Lord blessed the latter part of Job's life more than the former part."* Instead of 7,000 sheep, he now had 14,000! Instead of 3,000 camels he had 6,000! Instead of 500 oxen and donkeys he now had a 1000 of each! Job fathered ten more children who all grew to adulthood. And Job, honored by it all, lived such a long life that he saw his offspring down to the fourth generation! (42:10-17) The culmination of Job's life reminds me of Hebrews 10:35, which states, *"so do not throw away your confidence; it will be richly rewarded."* How encouraging!

This was the greater good that God always intended to accomplish through Job's suffering. Suffering challenges our faith to the core: It drives many of us to first question God, but later to trust and know him better. It is our journey through the "stages of faith" that mature our character, which is a great and gracious good.

What an important book Job is! It encourages us to not fall into self-righteousness as a result of suffering. It teaches us to avoid dogmatism in the foolish belief that we understand God. It reminds us that whether we understand or not, we can always trust our loving God fully. Such a God as ours is not to be doubted, only revered. He now has made clear many of his reasons for why he allowed Job to suffer. We do not need to know "all of those reasons" in order to give him all our trust. Job truly came to know the living God, not in spite of his suffering, but because of it. The suffering drove Job to his knees where he ultimately surrendered himself before his God. In complete trust, Job rested in him. His faith had been proved genuine!

APPENDIX A: THE PARALLELS OF JOB AND JESUS

Both Had Everything:

Job: Job 1:1-3

Jesus: John 1:1-2, 10, 14

Both Suffered The Loss Of Everything:

Job: Job 1:13-22

Jesus: Philippians 2:5-8; Luke 22:39; Isaiah 53:1-3

Both Were Tempted By Satan:

Job: Job 1:12-20

Jesus: Matthew 4:1-10; Isaiah 53:4-7

Both Were Falsely Accused Of Being Sinners:

Job: Job 4-31

Jesus: John 8:33-58

Both Suffered Though They Did Nothing Wrong:

Job: Job 1:21-22

Jesus: 1 Peter 2:21-23; Isaiah 53:9

Both Died Faithful To God:

Job: Job 42:16-17

Jesus: Luke 23:46… And so will we!

APPENDIX B: DISCIPLING PRACTICALS IN THE BOOK OF JOB

Lessons In Discipling Others

Positive reinforcement before challenges (4:1-11, 8:1-22)

Counsel from the Scriptures not opinions (4:12-21)

Explain the implications of sin (5:1-7)

Do not assume to know their heart (5:8-18)

Speak with faith and expect application (5:19-27)

Counsel to godly sorrow and encourage to seek input from others (8:5-10)

Do not belittle or become frustrated (8:1-7; 11:1-6; 15:1-6, 20:1-3)

Expect surrender and submission to God (22:21-28)

Lessons In Being Discipled

Be emotionally honest but do not lose hope in God's love (6:1-13, 7:1-21)

Seek input and appreciate the "silver lining" (6:14-24)

Have a submissive spirit without violating your conscience (6:24-30; 19:28-29; 27:1-6)

Remain teachable in the face of misunderstanding instead of self-righteous (27:11-12, 32:1)

Do not retaliate to sin but rather expose it (13:1-5, 16:1-5, 19:1-6, 21-22; 21:1-3,34; 26:1-4)

Seek the word and will of God at all costs (23:10-12; 28:12-28)

Remember that you are redeemed by God (16:15-21, 19:25-27)

Avoid justifying your actions (31)

Seek To First Understand And Not To Be Understood…

Be unbiased in your discipling of all parties (32:2-3, 15-22)

Always listen and give attention to all sides (32:10-14)

Age is not necessarily an indicator of superior wisdom (32:6-14)

Speak with authority but humility (33:1-7, 31-32)

Call out arrogance or self-pity (33:8-13)

Counsel to godly sorrow and repentance (33:14-18, 34:31-33)

Share the rewards of restoration (33:23-28)

Expose self-righteousness and entitlement (35:1-8)

Discipling must be based on the word of God and not opinion (36:1-4)

Remind them to love and fear God (36:5-12)

Warn them of the cost of bitterness, which can lead to evil (36:13-21)

Encourage them to stand in awe of God (36:22-37:24)

APPENDIX C: DISCIPLING & BEING DISCIPLED[20]

THE GOAL: Colossians 1:28-29

The goal of discipling is to present every Christian PERFECT in Christ.

Develop Christ-like attitudes and actions towards all aspects of life:

Your relationships

Your career

Helping the poor and under-privileged

Your finances

Evangelism, etc...

GOD'S PLAN: Jeremiah 17:9-10

Our own hearts deceive us therefore we all need DISCIPLING.

2 Samuel 12:1-13

Here is a classic example of the purpose and BENEFITS of having someone help us with our spiritual lives.

---

[20] *The Leaders' Resource Handbook. Volume 1.* Discipleship Publications International. (1998) P. 82-83

David is not dealing with his sin properly and it takes Nathan's words to get him honest and broken about what he has done.

Matthew 28:18-20

God wants every Christian to have someone in their lives teaching them to OBEY all of Jesus' commands.

THE DISCIPLER: 2 Corinthians 7:10-11

You must disciple to GODLY SORROW.

If people only have a worldly sorrow for their sin it will lead to spiritual death.

Therefore gently CONVICT people in your discipling do not just CONVINCE them.

Isaiah 28:27-29

Different people require different levels of hardness and tenderness: Cumin is a very soft seed, whereas grain has a hard outer shell. Therefore be sensitive and wise in your discipling of different people in different situations.

Galatians 6:1

If someone is CAUGHT in a sin restore them gently.

2 Corinthians 2:5-8

Comfort and re-affirm your love for someone to help them reach godly sorrow or else they may be overwhelmed with EXCESSIVE sorrow.

Proverbs 18:17

The first to present his case always seems right. Do not make judgments on issues until you have heard both sides of any story.

THE DISCIPLED: Proverbs 12:1

Your "Spiritual I.Q." is determined by your love for correction.

Rate yourself 1-10

Proverbs 12:15

Wise people SEEK ADVICE.

Proverbs 25:12

Rebukes should be seen as we would see "gifts of gold."

Proverbs 27:6

Disciples need to understand that counseling mistakes made by friends should be FORGOTTEN and FORGIVEN.

1 Corinthians 11:1

IMITATE the Christ-like qualities you see in your discipler.

THE END RESULT: Matthew 7:24-27

People who have been discipled to be like Christ and to put his words into practice will withstand the storms that beat against their faith and will IN THE END make it to Heaven.

APPENDIX D: DISCIPLING LEADERS OF THE FOUR BASIC TEMPERMENTS[21]

People are often divided into four basic "temperaments." Since there is a danger in categorization, realize that very often people have overlapping qualities. None of them are better or worse, only different; all have a valuable role in the kingdom. The goal is to be like Jesus; perfectly balanced in all areas.

So you need to be thankful for your strengths, excel in them, and use them for the kingdom. Work on your weaknesses, and strive for balance in your character.

Proverbs 20:5 – Respect and encourage others in their strengths. Identify and challenge others in their weaknesses. This is the essence of discipleship. It is the process of helping someone to grow into the image of Christ. (Colossians 1:28-29) Interestingly, our strengths in one situation will be our weakness in other situations.

What are some practical guidelines on how to disciple different temperaments?

A. Sanguine (Peter)

1. Leadership style: An influential individual who tends toward a persuasive style of leadership rather than an authoritative style.

2. Major needs (wants):

    a) Popularity

    b) Freedom

3. Biggest fear: Loss of social approval

4. Discipleship strategy:

a) ENCOURAGE:

1) Reassure them constantly of God's love and yours.

2) Build them up for their strengths, believe in and like them.

3) Be sure to build them up again after discipling them.

b) CHALLENGE:

1) They need high accountability.

2) Ask probing questions, as they tend to be secretive.

3) Challenge their pride and independence regularly.

5. Jesus with Peter: John 1:41-42; Matthew 16:13-23; John 21:15-22.

B. Choleric (Paul)

1. Leadership style: A dominant leader, forceful, authoritative, strong, opinionated –   very focused and driven, direct, high ego, impatient, desires change, progress and   success.

2. Major needs (wants):

a) A challenge (They love a stiff challenge.)

b) Authority (Significance, having an impact)

3. Biggest fear: Being taken advantage of

4. Discipleship strategy:

a) ENCOURAGE:

1) Let them lead something. Give them an opportunity. Solicit their input.

2) Inspire them by keeping the standard high and by being hard-line.

3) Reassure them of their impact. They need your respect!

    b) CHALLENGE:

1) "Overwhelm" them with responsibility so they will rely on God.

2) Help them to learn to meet the emotional needs of those they lead. Help them to get in touch with their own emotions regularly.

3) Challenge them to love and serve, and to not be domineering or Lord it over the people that they lead.

5. God/Jesus with Paul: Acts 22:6-15; 2 Corinthians 1:8-11; 2 Corinthians 12:7-10.

C. Phlegmatic (Timothy)

1. Leadership style: Steady, stabilizing influence; very family oriented – can be overly possessive, protective, but generally very loyal.

2. Major needs (wants):

    a) Security

    b) Acceptance

3. Biggest Fear: Loss of security or acceptance.

4. Discipleship Strategy:

    a) ENCOURAGE:

1) Value their friendship (John, "the apostle Jesus loved," was probably phlegmatic.) They are the most natural friends.

2) Reassure them of your friendship and loyalty to them.

3) Instill confidence in them.

b) CHALLENGE:

1) Teach them decisiveness, change! They tend to fear change in themselves and in their surroundings (discipling relationships, ministry, etc.)

2) Teach them to be dynamic and powerful.

3) Challenge laziness and complacency.

5. Paul with Timothy: 1 Timothy 1:1-4; 2 Timothy 1:2-12; 4:1-5

D. Melancholy (Moses)

1. Leadership style: Idealists, creative motivator, deep thinker and teacher, generally a very talented, competent, perceptive and compliant person – They appreciate accuracy and attention to detail.

2. Major needs (wants):

   a) Appreciation

   b) Friendship

3. Biggest fear: Being wrong

4. Discipleship strategy:

   a) ENCOURAGE:

1) Ask this person for their insights into things and share your own a lot. They enjoy and need deep conversation.

2) Take the time to find out what they are into and gain an appreciation for their expertise in that field. Encourage them about their creations regularly.

3) Teach them carefully and accurately by using the Bible quite often! Be patient with their questions and do not take that as being critical; they just need to know the reasons for things.

b) CHALLENGE:

1) Teach them that mistakes are okay. As perfectionists they need to hear about the grace of God, and your grace, over and over again.

2) Challenge them to by joyful always, as Philippians 4:4 commands.

3) Challenge them on their tendency to have a negative view of the world and their tendency to be down on themselves and others. This is very detrimental in discipling relationships, and they must learn to be positive, up on people, and not nitpicky in discipling relationships and marriage.

5. God with Moses: Exodus 3:1-21; 4:1-17

---

[21] *The Leaders Resource Handbook. Volume 1.* Discipleship Publications International. (1998) P. 82-84

Made in the USA
Monee, IL
27 July 2021